Bucking The System

Reclaiming Our Children's Minds
For Christ

Bucking The System

Bucking The System

Reclaiming Our Children's Minds
For Christ

Marisa Boonstra

ColRy Publishing

Bucking The System

Contact the Author:

email: marisa.boonstra@calledtomothering.com

Mailing Address:
Marisa Boonstra
12101 North MacArthur Boulevard
Suite 256
Oklahoma City, Oklahoma 73162

Bucking the System

Published by ColRy Publishing
A division of Vertical Vision, Inc.
12101 North MacArthur Boulevard
Suite 256
Oklahoma City, Oklahoma 73162

All scripture quotations, unless otherwise indicated, are taken from the Holy Bible, New American Standard Version® Copyright © 1960, 1962, 1963, 1968, 1971, 1972, 1973, 1975, 1977, 1995 by The Lockman Foundation Used by Permission

Copyright © 2016, 2018 by Marisa Boonstra

All rights reserved. No part of this book may be reproduced or transmitted in any form or by any means, electronic or mechanical, including photocopying and recording, or by any information storage and retrieval system, without permission in writing from the publisher.

Bucking The System
Reclaiming Our Children's Minds
For Christ

Bucking The System

Table of Contents

Introduction 9

Chapter 1: Competing Worldviews 17

Chapter 2: What Public Schools Are Really Teaching Our Children 31

Chapter 3: A History of Public Education in America 61

Chapter 4: Biblical Principles for Education 103

Chapter 5: Discovering a Better Way 123

For Further Reading 146

About The Author 147

Bucking The System

Introduction

Five years ago, I would not have batted an eye sending my children to public school. Like many Christian parents, I looked to this as not only a viable option for educating our kids, but also a very good one, providing we lived in a good district. When my son was a toddler, I would take him to the playground near the elementary school behind our house. I dreamed of the day he would be old enough to go there, because I loved learning growing up. I hoped it would be the same way for my son.

During the 12 years I spent in the public school system, I enjoyed the many friendships I made, was inspired by great teachers, and had fun being involved in choir and drama class. It gave me a great sense of community and identity. To say that I have an emotional connection to it would be an understatement. It was the biggest influence on me during my formative years.

Bucking The System

Looking back 18 years after graduating, I am not sure it was necessarily the best. The friendships, education, and fun activities all came at a high personal cost. There were peer pressure, bullies, cliques, and bad teachers/administration to contend with. The teachers that were good encouraged me academically, didn't make an impact where it counted the most, spiritually. I cared more about what my peers thought than my own parents and whatever values they and our church had instilled in me.

We lived in a mostly white, suburban neighborhood in one of the best districts in the state, but most of the kids were involved in some form of delinquency or another. In elementary and middle school, kids bullied and teased each other relentlessly. I had my share of "fair weather friends", and did my own teasing to gain the approval of my peers. By high school, many of us had tried alcohol, cigarettes, or even marijuana, and had engaged in premarital sex. A few girls had abortions, and several others had pregnancy scares. Two girls carried their babies to term and dropped out of school. All my friends who grew up in religious families that attended church on a regular basis, ended up becoming agnostic or atheist.

Everything that I learned in my classes and from my peers influenced my thinking and decisions. Though some of those influences were certainly positive, the overwhelming majority resulted in a marginal view of God and a low feeling of self worth. My values and morals slowly eroded over the years, leading to poor choices and heartbreak. By the time I reached college I was headed down a path of self destruction, which, if not for the grace of God, would have included promiscuity and alcoholism.

My family placed a big premium on education. My mother worked for the board of education in our district for 25 years. Eventually, my sister became a high school English teacher, and I chose a career as a School Social Worker. After making the switch to the child welfare system years later, I continued to engage with various schools on behalf of the foster kids I counseled.

In 2011, I began hearing about a disturbing education trend from some of my friends who had school-aged kids. Particularly in New York, Common Core was negatively impacting their children's interest in school and becoming a great cause for concern among these parents. Articles about the "trend" began popping up in my newsfeed, and even though my children were still a few years away from entering kindergarten, I started doing some research. What I discovered changed my entire perspective on the public education system.

As I descended into the rabbit hole of information about these new standards, I discovered more and more disturbing evidence of a much larger problem, of which Common Core is only a symptom. The public education system is, in fact, an institution of humanist values, philosophy, and ideas which are toxic to our children. It is not only failing them academically, but it is indoctrinating them into a worldview that is diametrically opposed to Biblical Christianity.

As parents who love the Lord and want our children to grow up loving Him as well, we protect them from the time they are born, throughout infancy into toddlerhood and then beyond into the preschooler stage. And then, at the ripe old age of 5 or 6, we hand them over to the public school system. A system full of teachings that mock everything we have painstakingly worked so hard to instill in our children. A system where they are not allowed to say God's name or learn what is in His word, for the sake of "tolerance".

We want our morals and values to be reinforced by those we entrust our children with for 6 hours a day, five days a week. We want the same messages to be taught by the other adults in their lives, the ones they look to for guidance, support, and education. If their teachers are not on the same page as we are, we will be fighting an uphill battle for at least the next 12 years and probably beyond that. We will have to undo nearly everything they are instructed to think, act, and experience because those things were not in line with our own values.

I look back and cringe at how my colleagues and I viewed the parents of the children we worked with in both the school and child welfare settings. In our meetings, we talked about them with contempt. They were seen as a nuisance, an interference in our work, instead of the most important and relevant authority. Our attitude was one of superiority; as the professionals, we knew what was best for children even more than their own parents.

Unfortunately, we live in a world now where teachers and social workers who work for the state have largely replaced the role of parents. The family is no longer the main institution of education, training, and discipline for children. It does not function as it was originally designed to by God. Parents have willingly abdicated their positions of authority to the "professionals." Boys and girls spend six to seven hours away from their mother and father, who are supposed to be their primary spiritual influences, each weekday in school. As a result, their peers have more influence on them than their parents do. As the family system only disintegrates farther, it becomes even more and more dependent on the government.

It begs the question, why? Why the breakdown in the family and the increase of society's reliance upon the welfare state? Martin Luther said, "I advise no one to place his child where the Scriptures do not reign paramount. Every institution in which men are not increasingly occupied with the Word of God must become corrupt... I am much afraid that schools will prove to be the great gates of hell unless they diligently labor in explaining the Holy Scriptures, engraving them in the hearts of youth." A person doesn't have to look very far to see that Scripture does not reign paramount in government run schools. If it is mentioned or discussed at all, it is only in a derogatory fashion, as though God's Word doesn't have any value to or bearing on students' modern education.

Imagine a school in which your child's main textbook is the Bible. Imagine that he or she filters everything they read, see, or hear through God's Word. How different would their perspectives be? How much better equipped would our youth be to defend their faith to a secular culture? How different would our society be? We need to remember the wise words of Proverbs 1:7, "The fear of the Lord is the beginning of knowledge", and return to God's original design for the education of our children.

My people are destroyed for lack of knowledge. - Hosea 4:6

Bucking The System

Chapter 1: Competing Worldviews

A 2006 study by The Barna Group showed that despite strong levels of spiritual activity during the teen years, 70-75% of Christian youth leave the church visible after high school.[1] In total, six out of ten twenty-somethings were involved in a church during their teen years, but have failed to translate that into active spirituality during their early adulthood. Those are not just troubling statistics; this is indicative of an epidemic!

Pastors and youth ministry workers have been trying to figure out how to solve this problem for years. They say better youth ministries are needed, that include both discipleship and relevant messages. They look towards the parents' active, committed faith as being a deciding factor whether the church retains its youth. They declare that children's programs need to be better at teaching solid biblical truths. These are all very good things that are definitely needed, but I believe we are looking in the wrong place. We have to seriously consider the importance of input.

---

[1] https://www.barna.org/barna-update/millennials/147-most-twentysomethings-put-christianity-on-the-shelf-following-spiritually-active-teen-years#.VoNF47YrKt9

Bucking The System

Ideas and philosophies which are contrary to God's Word come from two main pipelines: secular entertainment and secular education. As Christians, we do a pretty good job at stemming the tide of entertainment's influence on our children. We all know the children's song: "Be careful little ears what you hear..." We have taken that to heart on the matter of secular entertainment. Most of us would never dream of putting our children in front of television shows, movies, video games, and music that contain harmful influences to their spiritual development for the majority of their waking hours. Yet that is exactly what we do when we place them in government run schools.

The National Education Association (NEA), the largest labor union in the United States, representing public school teachers, faculty and staff at colleges and universities, plus retired educators, has been criticized over the last three decades for failing students academically. Criticism has contained a litany of problems including decreasing test scores, poor academic performance, high dropout rates, ineffective curriculums, student violence, and even low teacher morale. The NEA's solutions have been more money for education, better health plans, small class size, higher teacher pay, new buildings, new curricula, more computers, etc. None of these have worked to improve the academia of American children. In fact, a 2011 report by the U.S. Department of Education showed that despite the massive increase in spending, student test results have stayed about the same or even got worse.[2]

    Author and educator, Dr. Samuel Blumenfeld, confirmed that government schools are not actually educating but in fact indoctrinating when he wrote in an article for *The New American* titled "Colonial Education: Superior to Today's Public Schools" on February 24, 2011, "The drugging of over four million children by their educators to cure Attention Deficit Disorder, a steep decline in literacy, and an anti-Christian philosophy of education [is what the American people are getting for their tax money.]" He went on to say that if it weren't for the growth of the homeschool movement... the country would in time become a totalitarian society controlled by behavioral psychologists and corrupt politicians.

    The 1962 Supreme Court Case of Engel v. Vitale made it illegal to pray in school. One year later

---

[2] David Fiorazo, "Eradicate: Blotting Out God In America" (Abbotsford, WI: Life Sentence Publishing), 2012.

another case, Abington School District v. Schempp, ruled that school-sponsored Bible reading was unconstitutional. Justice Potter Stewart, the one dissenting vote in both cases, blasted the ruling saying, "It led not to true neutrality with respect to religion, but to the establishment of a religion of secularism." Contrary to popular belief, education is *not* religiously neutral. If God and His Word have been blotted out of modern public schools (and they have), then they have been replaced with another god and another- false- gospel. Although made up of individual teachers, or even principals, who may happen to be Christians, the public school is by and large a system, one that teaches a worldview that is directly opposed to Biblical Christianity.

A worldview is a set of beliefs about God, man, knowledge, ethics, and truth. It is the lens through which a person views and processes information. It is the reason that people can defend abhorrent things like abortion and suicide bombings. Voddie Baucham, in his 2007 book *Family Driven Faith*, says a child's world view affects all of their decisions and actions throughout their lives. What people believe ultimately effects how they behave.

A child's world view is also formed informally, and uncritically. Children do not realize or recognize when or how these views are being formed, and the government schools intentionally take advantage of this when children are young, establishing foundational thinking for their whole life. "Education is the most powerful ally of Humanism, and every American public school is a school of Humanism," Charles Francis Potter wrote in his 1930 book, *Humanism: A New Religion*.

From evolution in Science classes to transcendentalism in English classes, the philosophy of Secular Humanism makes its way into the heart and minds of our children from a very early age. Secular Humanism is the belief that there is no God, and that humans are ever evolving and becoming "enlightened". It declares that knowledge is limited to the world that the human senses can perceive. It denies that there has been any supernatural revelation given to man, so man's only means of discovering truth is through human reason by use of the scientific method. Humanism also perceives that man is essentially good and perfectable; therefore it expects continued progress to a more perfect order on earth.[3] Post-modern thought, such as moral relativism, was born out of this worldview. It was recognized as an official religion by the United States Supreme Court in the 1961 case of Torcaso v. Watkins.

This religion replaces God with man as the ultimate authority in the universe. The Word of God is replaced by man's ability to observe and reason. God's law is replaced by moral relativity. Sin is replaced by anything that prevents man from fulfilling his man-given purpose of living for one's own pleasure and self-fulfillment, the lust of the flesh, the lust of the eyes, and the pride of life (1 John 2:16). Hell is replaced by failure to fulfill one's man-given purpose. Finally, the gospel is replaced by having faith in yourself instead of God and doing whatever it takes to achieve your "salvation", even if it violates God's law.

The educational system of the state, by their own admission, is not neutral and teaches a religion opposed to Christianity. "I am convinced that the battle for humankind's future must be waged and won in the public school classroom by teachers who correctly

---

[3] Renald Showers, "What On Earth Is God Doing: Satan's Conflict With God" (Neptune, New Jersey: Loizeaux Brothers, Inc.), 1973.

perceive their role as the proselytizers of a new faith: a religion of humanity that recognizes and respects the spark of what theologians call divinity in every human being. *These teachers must embody the same selfless dedication as the most rabid fundamentalist preachers, for they will be ministers of another sort, utilizing a classroom instead of a pulpit to convey humanist values in whatever subject they teach,* regardless of the educational level—preschool day care or large state university. The classroom must and will become an arena of conflict between the old and the new—the rotting corpse of Christianity, together with all its adjacent evils and misery, and the new faith of humanism."[4]

It should be both eye-opening and chilling to know that the father of modern American education, John Dewey, was such a proponent of Humanism. He once said, "There is no God and no soul. Hence, there are no needs for the props of traditional religion. With dogma and creed excluded, then immutable (unchangeable) truth is also dead and buried. There is no room for fixed, natural law, or permanent moral

---

[4] John Dunphy, "A Religion for a New Age", Humanist, Jan.-Feb. 1983, p. 26

absolutes." It is therefore not shocking that the sentiment "God is dead" runs rampant among graduates of the public schools today. It is all about out with the old Christianity, in with the new Humanism.

What does the effect of this type of teaching have on young students? Essentially, they are being trained in an anti-Christian environment. Child Psychologist Frederick Wortham said, "A child's mind is like a bank. Whatever goes into it comes back ten years later with interest." If our children sit under this teaching for twelve to thirteen foundational years of their life (14,000 seat hours worth of time), their worldview will be cemented in Secular Humanism by the time they graduate high school, despite all of our efforts to pour the Word of God into their lives.

Plainly speaking, whoever disciples the child will have his heart. Matthew 6:40 says, "A pupil is not above his teacher; but everyone, after he has been fully trained, will be like his teacher." The one who teaches a child (the "system" or curriculum, not necessarily the individual) forms that child's worldview. Children will ultimately default to the worldview they have been exposed to the most during their youth.

In order for a child to establish deep roots of faith, he or she needs to grow inside of an environment that has the conditions necessary to cultivate it. The "soil" of the public school with all of its humanistic teachings is hostile to that young seed. In time, the plant develops weak roots or completely withers and dies. Jesus illustrated the importance of a believer having deep roots in the Parable of the Sower in Matthew 13. For children, it is even more important because of their nature to soak up any kind of information without straining out that which contradicts biblical teaching.

Widely syndicated columnist Cal Thomas, on the issue of sex and drug use in public schools, stated, "Step one is to pull them [kids] from the government schools that serve as hothouses for this kind of behavior and thinking... The government schools and the sex and entertainment industries aren't about to fix the problem. The responsibility to properly raise children belong to parents. The state and various interest groups have no right to develop the moral fiber of a child, and in fact, they are speedily undermining that development." The solution he proposes to these problems is almost too simple: remove kids from the environment that breeds these types of immorality. More drug or sex "education" in public schools will not and cannot solve the problem.

Bucking The System

For Christian parents, how much time is realistically spent countering the public school system's teaching in their limited amount of time at home with their children, after homework, sports, and other extracurricular activities? Just to be generous, if parents spent 30 minutes a day year-round teaching their child from Scripture, plus the child received 1 hour per week in Sunday school, that would equal only 2,366 hours to try to counteract the 14,000 the anti-Christian schools are teaching. To get that much instruction from church, a child would have to attend two hours a week for one hundred and forty years![5] Is it any wonder that most children who were raised in Christian homes and grew up going to church reject their parents' beliefs and ultimately end up abandoning the faith?

One of the reasons we are losing the culture war is because many of us do not understand how critical Christian education is, in the evangelism and discipleship of the next generation. Muslims acknowledge the importance of education in the conversion of young people to Islam. Sheikh Ahmad Al Katani, in an interview on the Al Jazeera television

---

[5] http://exodusmandate.org/public-schools/top-five-reasons-not-to-send-your-kids-back-to-public-school

network, responded to the fact that six million African Muslims are being converted to Christianity each year. He said, "You have to build the worshipper before you build the mosque. Schools should be built first, which are the primary source of spreading Islam and to protect the Muslim... We are proud of the mosque, but had we used the money to build a school, it would have been a lot more beneficial." The Sheikh realized that the best way to counteract the Christian influence on Muslims was to establish schools rooted in the Islamic faith. The reason for millions of converts in the first place? Not large evangelistic crusades, but Christian education!

An article by Jonathan Lewis in the Sept.-Oct. 2014 issue of *Home School Enrichment* tells the story of a Hindu mother who sent her daughter to a small Christian school. This mother was initially perplexed by her daughter's repeated references to the Bible, wondering how a one-hour Bible class per day could spark such an interest. When her daughter's teacher informed her that she tried to teach about the Bible all day long- not just during the regular Bible class- the light went on, and the mother went from perplexed to distressed. "How can I compete with that?" she exclaimed. This Hindu mother realized what many

Christian parents need to understand; the worldview of our children's education matters.

"To think we can win the culture war when a majority of Christian children are still being indoctrinated in the public schools doesn't pass the common sense test, much less the theology test," founder and president of Frontline Ministries, Inc. and director of the Exodus Mandate Project, E. Ray Moore says. If it strikes us as odd that a Hindu parent would choose a Christian school and then be surprised when her child shows an interest in Christianity, why is it that so many Christian parents send their children to a secular school and then are surprised when their children actually become secular? If our goal is to raise children who understand a biblical worldview and are shaped more by God's Word than the philosophies of the world, we should choose a process of education that is consistent with that goal.

No academic skepticism, no secularist authors, no blatant materialism can so undermine the spiritual life of the country like the completely secularized training of the child under the authority of the state.[6] Anybody can see that America is steadily heading down

---

[6] http://daveblackonline.com/our.htm

a steep embankment of moral decline. We cannot be shocked when we input humanistic teachings into children's minds all these years, and the outcome is a nation full of atheists. Well-known Baptist preacher and theologian Charles Spurgeon once said, "The only way to keep chaff out of the child's cup is to fill it brimful with good wheat." God's Word has been tossed out of public schools, and with it, the morals of three generations of Americans.

Bucking The System

Chapter 2: What Public Schools Are Really Teaching Our Children

When most people think of humanist ideas being taught in school they concentrate mainly on evolution, which, they reason, is limited only to the subject of Science. It is the most obvious toxin to Christian parents, as it clearly opposes the Creation account in Genesis. However, it cannot be neatly categorized as a topic relegated to just one academic subject; it is a belief that underscores all the other subjects. Renowned secular humanist Sir Julian Huxley said that the keynote, central concept to which all of humanism's details are related is evolution.[7]

If a person accepts evolution as fact, he or she reaches one of two conclusions. First, not being able to reconcile the struggle and waste of the evolutionary process with the existence of a good and sovereign Creator, they conclude that there is no God.[8] Second, believing that evolution is the way that God used to

---

[7] http://www.truthmagazine.com/archives/volume30/GOT030254.html

[8] John Dillenberger & Claude Welch, "Protestant Christianity: Interpreted Through Its Development" (New York, NY: Scribners), 1955.

create and maintain life, they conclude God works within natural processes instead of by miraculous intervention in the natural order. Both conclusions lead to the belief that the Bible is not divinely inspired, therefore it has little relevance to people's lives. Christianity, the Bible, and the One True God are simply evolutionary developments of man's religious consciousness.[9] With religion being in a constant state of development, there can be no such thing as moral absolutes, either.

Despite the fact that evolution has not and cannot be proven by observable scientific methods, it is taught as undisputed fact in the public schools. "I will not accept that [creation] philosophically, because I do not want to believe in God. Therefore, I choose to believe in that which I know is scientifically impossible, spontaneous generation arising to evolution," Nobel Prize Winner George Wald wrote in *Biochemical Science: An Inquiry Into Life*. Sir Arthur Keith, in the forward to the 100th anniversary edition of Darwin's book *Origin of Species*, says "Evolution is unproved and unprovable. We believe it only because the only

---

[9] Earle E. Cairns, "Christianity Through The Centuries: A History of the Christian Church" (Grand Rapids, MI: Zondervan), 2000.

alternative is special creation, and that is unthinkable." Even evolutionists concede that evolutionary theory is unscientific, yet creationism is not allowed to be taught in government schools as an alternative.

In reality, a belief in evolution has little to do with science, and everything to do with an unbelief in, or rather hostility to, God the Creator. Evolution and Humanism go hand in hand. Humanistic philosophy is woven through each of the academic subjects in public school, making it impossible to carefully select one topic or curriculum for your child to avoid. Let's take a look at how the beliefs that flow from Humanism specifically frame each subject, and their implications for a youth's understanding of God.

Science

Believing that humans are the direct descendants of primates, not created in the image of God, students conclude they have no real purpose in life except to live their lives for their own pleasure and self-fulfillment. At best, human life and animal life are viewed as having equal value, and at worst, humans are a cancer that must be removed from this planet for the sake of the environment. God is kicked off of His throne in place of man; and man becomes the supreme being of the universe with the "divine" right to determine what is true according to what seems right in his own eyes. This view ultimately leads to freedom of conscience before a holy and just God. Sin is seen as only an animal instinct in man.

Environmentalism has become a popular subject in the classroom, teaching students that man is taking up valuable resources on the planet, dangerously elevating the worth of plants and animals over that of human beings. Tom DeWeese, writing for *Worldview Times*, stated "in short, the modern environmental movement was chosen as the shock and awe tactic to force America into the global village. Over the next three decades these forces combined to rapidly and drastically change America in a very significant way... Change the attitudes, values and beliefs of just one generation and America will forget its founding principles and fall in line with the globalist worldview." Conservationism is the highest ideal among people these days, and global warming and overpopulation have somehow become scientific realities, even though they cannot be proven scientifically.

Overpopulation is a theory that Thomas Malthus constructed in the late 1700's. Malthus was an English scholar and mathematician who believed "the power of population is indefinitely greater than the power in the earth to produce subsistence for man." He was influential in raising economic fears of overpopulation and concerns about a shortage of food and resources, which later proved to be unfounded. Malthus believed in the survival of the fittest and that the poor were not worth feeding, and unfortunately, his ideas still persist today among proponents of both evolution and abortion.

History

History is not taught as being controlled by God, but rather as a series of events directed by the will of man. History classes reject the historical dates given in the Bible for important events and figures, leading students to have a faulty understanding of the beginning of key civilizations and the nature of man. History is divided into different periods such as the Cosmological (origin of universe), Geological (origin of earth), Prehistoric Period (origin of man, before recorded history), and Historical (written history). The Prehistoric Period is broken down into the stone age, ice age, bronze age, and iron age, because man is seen as continually evolving.

The timeline given generally goes something like the following. The earth was formed approximately 4.5 billion years ago, supposedly evidenced from radiometric dating. 200 million years ago, dinosaurs and other prehistoric animals roamed the earth. 2 million years ago, after all the dinosaurs had died out, the first man called "homo erectus" appeared in Africa. He developed from a monkey, and began living in caves.

These "cave men" were unintelligent and did not know how to make many things or know how to reason. They are often portrayed as men and women who act more like animals than humans. Eventually, they figured out how to make primitive tools out of animal bones and stones. During the Stone Age of human development, the earth also experienced an Ice Age some 1.6 million to 10,000 years ago. Then thousands of years later, they learned how to make tools out of bronze. Finally, in 1300 BC, the ability to extract and work with iron developed.

Ancient History courses teach Mesopotamia as the first civilization, because it had the first form of observable writings, but ignore the precursors of Adam and Eve, their descendants, Noah, The Flood, or the Tower of Babel as recorded in Genesis. The Patriarchs' and Israelites' place in and contribution to history are minimized and glossed over, while those of Ancient

Egypt, India, China, Babylon, Persia, Greece, and Rome are highlighted extensively.

When students try to overlap the Bible's explanation in Genesis of the beginning of time with the one learned in school, they find that the two do not fit together. In fact, they are usually so drastically different that it leads students to the conclusion that Scripture, rather than man, is inaccurate. Also, "B.C.E." meaning "before the common era" is now used in place of the abbreviation "B.C.", for dates that occurred before Christ's birth. As a result, Jesus Christ is no longer viewed and respected as the apex of history.

Any sign of Christianity's positive impact on modern civilization is virtually non-existent. For over 225 years, the greatest influence on our country has been the Gospel. Brave pioneering settlers fought the elements and illnesses to arrive on its shores so they could freely worship God. Children will not learn in public school, however, that most of America's Founding Fathers were theologically trained and founded the nation on biblical principles. They, along with the original settlers, The Puritans, are demonized as murdering bigots for "stealing land from the Native Americans" and owning slaves.

Even though most of the primary documents from the Founding Fathers are full of references to God and direct quotes from the Bible, demonstrating that our country was indeed founded upon Christian principles, the public school history curriculum pretends that these documents never existed. Instead, things like "separation of church and state" are taught when there is no mention of any such separation in the United States Constitution. This phrase comes from one sentence in a letter by Thomas Jefferson to the Danbury Baptists, written in 1802. Author and historian David Barton states that Jefferson believed God, not government, was the author and source of our rights. The idea was to prevent government from interfering with those rights. He explained, "Very simply, the "wall of separation" in the Danbury letter was not to limit religious activities in public; rather they were to limit the power of the government to prohibit or interfere with those expressions."[10]

Students no longer study the Constitution, or memorize the Declaration of Independence and The Gettysburg Address. They are taught that America is a

---

[10] David Fiorazo, "Eradicate: Blotting Out God In America" (Abbotsford, WI: Life Sentence Publishing), 2012.

democracy, instead of a republic. John Adams once said, "We are a nation of laws, not of men", meaning that our rights come from God, and not legislators. A democracy is government operated and ruled by direct majority vote of the people. The majority calls the shots on policy matters through public meetings or by voting on referendums. A republic, however, is where the general population elects leaders to represent them, who, in turn, make policy decisions on their behalf and then pass laws to govern.

In addition, Social Studies classes teach every religion as basically having equal value and that every spiritual path leads to eternal life. Jesus is referenced as just another prophet, or good teacher, who began a religion based on "love and tolerance". There is little said about the fact that He claimed to be the Son of God. No distinction is made between Christianity's way of achieving salvation (believing in a Savior who did the work of atonement for us) and other religions' ways (doing enough good works).

The only time Christianity is mentioned is to highlight the arrogance and atrocities of the Crusades, the Inquisition, or the Salem Witch Trials. Christians are portrayed throughout history as judgmental, self-righteous, unloving, and hypocritical, chastised for trying to legislate morality. The Crusades are treated as a purely offensive set of battles, when in fact, they were a reaction to the violent Islamic takeover of previously Christian lands. Many of the key battles are omitted from textbooks, even though they were critical in stopping the Muslim conquests from spreading westward and preserving Western civilization.

The textbooks on average devote far more space to Islam than to other faiths.[11] They portray Islam as a religion tolerant of other faiths, even though of the forty-one Islamic countries in the world, freedom of religion is found in only four. Textbooks state that peace-loving Muslims are the controlling faction within their faith, while radical terrorists are outliers, making up only a small percentage. Chapters on Islam rarely mention the Jihadist element, or mention how violent sects control nearly all the major mosques, schools, and foundations within the Islamic world. They also fail to mention the dozens of passages in the Koran calling for the elimination of infidels (anyone who is not a Muslim).

The Council on Islamic Education (CIE), an anti-West, anti-Israel group, focuses exclusively on

---

[11] Steven Baldwin & Karen Holgate, "From Crayons To Condoms: The Ugly Truth About America's Public Schools", (Washington, D.C.: WND Books), 2008.

influencing school textbooks. It has been reported that CIE's board members have made false statements such as "American children need to know that genocide was part of the birth of this nation" and have boasted that its efforts to influence textbooks is the equivalent of waging a "bloodless" revolution.[12] Textbook publishers such as Houghton Mifflin, Teachers Curriculum Institute, Scott Foresman, and Glencoe & Prentice Hall openly list CIE as an organization they consult with when writing sections on Islam.

Pagan beliefs, mysticism, and even witchcraft have made their way into Social Studies classes, under the guise of teaching children to appreciate other cultures and religions. Students are taught to alter their consciousness through centering exercises, guided imagery, and visualizations in self-esteem, multicultural, and arts programs. After studying a pagan myth, students are often asked to imagine or visualize a dream or vision, then describe it in a journal or lesson assignment. Countless teachers across the country require students to document their daily horoscopes. Through palmistry, I Ching, tarot cards, and

---

[12] Steven Baldwin & Karen Holgate, "From Crayons To Condoms: The Ugly Truth About America's Public Schools" (Washington, D.C.: WND Books), 2008.

horoscopes, students supposedly learn to experience other cultures and tap into secret sources of wisdom. Students in Texas were told to create a vision in their minds and "describe in your best soothsayer tones the details of your vision."[3]

While pagan myths and crafts show students how to contact ancestral, nature, and other spirits, classroom rituals actually invoke their presence. California third-graders were given an assignment to alter their consciousness through guided imagery, invoking their personal animal spirits. They were then supposed to write about their experience and create their own magical medicine shields to represent their "spirit helper."

Gullible students from coast to coast are learning the ancient formulas and occult techniques of magic, spells, and sorcery. They learn about such occult charms and symbols as Dreamcatchers, Zuni fetishes, crystals, and power signs like the quartered circle and Hindu mandala. After seating themselves "according to their astrological signs," Oregon students, who traded Christmas for a Winter Solstice celebration, watched

---

[3] http://exodusmandate.org/public-schools/public-schools-pagan-religion-indoctrination-centers

the "sun god" and "moon goddess" enter the auditorium to the beating of drums and chanting. Most of disturbing of all, students get lessons about pagan societies' appreciation for the "unifying power of promiscuity." By studying these pagan notions on sexuality, children get the idea that promiscuity is normal and acceptable.

Teaching pagan beliefs and religions can harm children. Author Aldous Huxley wrote about 'new-think' indoctrination in Brave New World, his frightening novel about a future totalitarian society. In his book, school authorities molded children's minds so that as adults, they lost their ability to think critically or judge the policies of their leaders. Indoctrinating children with pagan beliefs in our public schools could have a similar effect. If a child believes he or she can turn into a bird or pass a math test by rubbing a voodoo necklace, then facts, reason, hard work, and dedication go out the window.

English

Many English classes continue the assault on Christianity by teaching students how to interpret literature from a deconstructionalist point of view. This process of interpretation typically involves demonstrating the multiple possible readings of a text.

It is more commonly known as whole language. Through this method, "meaning is created through a *transaction* with whole, meaningful texts... It is a transaction, not an extraction of the meaning from the print... reading is not a matter of 'getting the meaning' from text, as if that meaning were in the text waiting to be decoded by the reader."[14] With this view of textual interpretation, there is no single correct meaning for a given book or novel. This results in students who read asking themselves the question "what does the text mean to me?", instead of "what does the text actually mean?"

As a result, when Christian public school students go to the Bible and approach its interpretation in the same way, they end up with the hermeneutical error of isogesis. This is when a reader's opinions are forced upon the scriptures resulting in the reader reading into the text whatever he wants the text to say, instead of using proper exegetical hermeneutics to find out what the text actually means. Isogesis not only results in an inaccurate interpretation of scripture, but

---

[14] Bess Altweger, Carole Edelsky, and Barbara Flores, "Whole Language, What's the Difference?" (Portsmouth, NH: Heinemann), 1991.

the reader also becomes guilty of placing his opinions in authority over God's Word.

The illogical nature of whole language is simply an expression of the humanist philosophy that dominates public education, which is that there is no absolute moral truth. As a result, each individual person determines "truth" according to what seems right in his own eyes. Situational ethics are taught in both English and History classes. In light of moral relativism, the situation a person is in would determine whether what that person did was good or evil. With this worldview, it is possible for obvious evils like cold blooded murder, adultery, theft, lying, and cheating to be viewed as morally good if it accomplishes what a person would consider to be a "good" end.

This is how students ultimately justify using evil means in the name of self-fulfillment, or even justify calling what is obviously evil good, like abortion. Isaiah 5:20 says, "Woe to those who call evil good, and good evil; who substitute darkness for light and light for darkness; who substitute bitter for sweet and sweet for bitter!" According to the 2010 Josephson Institute of Ethics' Survey, even though the majority of these children demonstrated an undeniable lack of integrity, 92% were completely satisfied with their personal ethics and character. By eliminating Almighty God from their worldview, they have eliminated the only possible source of absolute truth. With no source for absolute truth, they conclude that absolute truth must not exist, and as a result, each individual person is left to determine truth for himself. The social repercussions of such a philosophy are either anarchy or totalitarianism, when for the sake of an orderly society, the strong impose their "morality" and views of "truth" on the rest of the population.

Much of the literature included in public school English curricula was written by atheists, whose humanist worldview formed their writing. Well-known authors such as Ayn Rand, Jean-Paul Sartre, H.G. Wells and others wrote novels depicting stories and characters with a godless, apathetic view on life. Their works have influenced millions of people, including impressionable youth that read them in classrooms across the country.

In addition, many of the books that students are required to read, including many of the so called "classics", teach doctrines that are either contrary to Scripture or deliberately paint Biblical Christianity in a bad light. For example, Nathaniel Hawthorne's *The Scarlet Letter* raises the tolerance of sin to the level of a virtue and unjustly portrays the Puritans, and in the mind of public school students, all Christians as tyrannical, cruel, judgmental, and narrow-minded. In another example, students read the works of Transcendentalists like Thoreau and Emerson, who teach ideas that are similar to today's New Age spirituality.

    Instead of reading about brave missionaries like Jim Elliott, David Livingstone, William Carey, and Amy Carmichael who risk their lives to share the gospel with unreached people groups, they read books like *Things Fall Apart* by Chinua Achebe. In Achebe's novel, missionaries are portrayed as disruptive to and unappreciative of the African culture of the people they witness to. The main character tells the story of how his tribe's way of life disintegrates, and he loses many of the people he loves to the white men's strange new religion. By the end of the book, he is so distraught that he kills himself. This leaves the reader to conclude that missions work is destructive. It does not highlight the benevolence of missionaries which includes setting up schools and hospitals, and also distributing food and clean water to the people they tell about Jesus. The book leaves out the fact that many tribesmen who convert to Christianity were once enslaved to spirit worship and a life of extreme violence. Because of their fearful beliefs, they rely upon witch doctors, who often prey on the people's superstitious nature by making them pay exorbitant amounts of money to "heal" illnesses and "bring" rain.

In addition, books with filthy language, violence, and explicit sex are assigned to students as young as middle school. Many of these novels feature main characters who engage in incredibly risky behavior and suffer only minimal consequences for their actions. These books also include very dark themes such as addiction, suicide, sexual abuse, and even demon possession. Scenes contained within them are often graphically portrayed and totally inappropriate for minors. The stories have little redemptive value, with evil usually triumphing over good.

Of particular concern is the inclusion of lessons on "death education". Students are given assignments such as the "Fallout Shelter", where they are supposed to choose whom they would save from a catastrophic event based on a person's characteristics and behavior. Here, children are essentially asked to rate the quality of other people's lives. Some lives are inevitably deemed not as worthy and do not "make the cut". Students are also instructed to write their own obituary using a scenario in which a family member caused their death. Not only does this inappropriate lesson place an unhealthy emphasis on dying, it hints that family should not be trusted and undermines familial bonds.

The increase in the presence of this dangerous curriculum may be contributing to the climbing suicide rates among teenagers. When teachers who are untrained in the field of mental health handle psychologically sensitive topics with their students, it can be disastrous to children that are at-risk. Exploring such potentially explosive subjects in an unsafe environment like a classroom, instead of in a therapeutic setting, could lead to an unstable child believing that death is a viable option to solving his or her problems. This unhealthy preoccupation with dying through various books and assignments is the natural result of removing any semblance of God from public schools. As God Himself said, "all who hate Me love death." (Proverbs 8:36b)

Sex Education

Perhaps the most insidious of all subjects taught in government school is "sex education". The textbooks and manuals for this curriculum list consultants such as NARAL (National Abortion Rights Action League),

Planned Parenthood, and Guttmacher Institute, powerful abortion lobbies. Planned Parenthood, America's biggest abortion provider, created sex education programs for students in grades K-12 under the auspices of a "safe sex" philosophy. It continues to fund these programs nationwide, and reaps the business from hundreds of thousands of vulnerable young women seeking abortions each year.

 The abortion industry's leader essentially created a problem where there wasn't one, and stepped in to provide the solution. Many people today believe that sex education is the only way to stop the spread of teen pregnancy and disease, when in fact it is the main cause of these epidemics. Planned Parenthood still boasts that they do more than anyone else to prevent unwanted pregnancies and sexually transmitted diseases, but a 2008 report by the Centers for Disease Control found that more than one in four (26%) teenage girls between the ages of 14 and 19 are infected with the four most common STDs. Planned Parenthood's response to the CDC's report was simply that more "comprehensive sex education" is needed.

 Twenty-two percent of all pregnancies (excluding miscarriages) end in abortion, and at current rates, 1 in 10 women will have an abortion by age 20, 1 in

4 by age 30, and 3 in 10 by age 45.39.[15] These statistics reflect the general attitude that exists within the public school student culture that abortion is just another birth control option. To them, murdering their unborn babies is preferable to taking responsibility for their actions, and Planned Parenthood is all too willing to "counsel" them to make the problem go away. Many teenage boys see abortion as their "get out of jail free card" from the responsibility of fatherhood and as a license to pursue a promiscuous lifestyle, while many of the teenage girls see abortion as a feminist right and the key to liberate themselves from the "shackles" of motherhood.

    The numbers indicate that sex education is not effective. Instead of a reduction in teen pregnancy and STDs, these have actually skyrocketed over the last twenty years. Curricula does not promote the avoidance of high risk sex, but rather teaches how to engage in high risk sex in allegedly safer ways, continuing to push the envelope of "acceptable" forms of intimate expression. Margaret Sanger, the founder of Planned Parenthood, once stated that her primary goal was not to encourage marriage, but rather "increase the

---

[15] Answers Magazine, Vol. 8 No. 2, April – June 2013, p. 13.

quantity and quality of sexual relationships." She wrote in her 1922 book, *The Woman Rebel,* "Our objective is unlimited sexual gratification without the burden of unwanted children... Women have the right live... to love... to be an unmarried mother... to create... to destroy... The marriage bed is the most degenerative influence in the social order."

Sex talks in high schools across the nation, provided by Planned Parenthood, encourage students to be dishonest with their parents. PP's employees tell teenage girls that they can get birth control without the consent or knowledge of their parents, and promise that they themselves will not even report this information to parents! Their "education" involves the sexualization of young kids and teens, then selling them birth control, and when they catch an STD, selling them testing services. When a young girl inevitably becomes pregnant, they then sell her an abortion. It's a win-win for Planned Parenthood, and a lose-lose proposition for impressionable youth.

Shockingly, with all of the crude information students receive, representatives from the National Education Association (NEA) say one of the problems with education today is kids aren't taught enough about sex. They actually believe that oral sex, masturbation, and orgasms need to be taught in the classroom! Are these the kind of people we want choosing curriculum for our children? Various textbooks and manuals have endorsed prostitution, anal sex, same-sex marriages, pornography, and even incest. Indeed, a study of the sex education leadership by the Institute for Media Education has found that a large number of the leaders of the movement are admitted pedophiles, have publicly advocated sex between children and adults, or are actively involved in the pornography industry.[16]

    A relatively new form of sex education called HIV/AIDS Education endorses and promotes the homosexual lifestyle, to children as young as kindergarten. The Diversity Resolution makes it clear that schools are to teach about sexual orientation and gender identification to students in all grades. One of the NEA's goals is changing public opinion on homosexuality, starting with the youngest generation. Under the guise of "safe schools", public schools should raise awareness of homophobia and intervene when LGBT students are harassed. Elementary school students are asked questions of a sexual nature in

---

[16] Steven Baldwin & Karen Holgate, "From Crayons To Condoms: The Ugly Truth About America's Public Schools" (Washington, D.C.: WND Books), 2008.

surveys, to determine "psychological barriers to learning".

The homosexual lobby helped get Bill Clinton elected as president in 1992 in return for his promises to further their agenda in public schools. When President Clinton spoke at the 1993 NEA convention, he confirmed their partnership and actually told the audience his "goals for America closely parallel those of the NEA." Gay, Lesbian, and Straight Teachers Network introduced a resolution at the Minneapolis convention that same year, which introduced "the celebration of a Lesbian and Gay History Month as a means of acknowledging the contributions of lesbians, gays, and bisexuals throughout history."

A Day of Silence (DOS) was started in 1996, a full day dedicated to raising awareness about bullying and hate, primarily stifling any student who might believe homosexuality is wrong. On this day in public school across the country, a pro-gay message is often sent to the students, with teachers and administrators frequently promoting homosexuality, bisexuality, and transgenderism over the course of the school day. Linda Harvey, founder of the Christian pro-family Mission America, writes that the goal for DOS is to "exploit the tender sympathies of kids to promote approval of homosexuality and gender confusion." Schools teach that Judeo-Christian morality is the enemy of homosexuals and gender-confused people, because it silences and persecutes them. The conclusion reached by students is that traditional moral beliefs cause bullying.

An LGBT trainer for the NEA, Diane Schneider, in speaking to a panel against homophobia, said that the association opposed abstinence-based sex education. She also implied family and religion are two things that hold back the advancement of homosexuality. Incredulously, she stated that comprehensive sex education is the only way to combat heterosexism and gender conformity. As a result, the institutions of marriage and family as designed by God, are shattered in public schools.

The Gay, Lesbian and Straight Education Network (GLSEN) recommends books for teachers on down to grade-schoolers, encouraging the sexualization of children regardless of "orientation". This organization was founded by Kevin Jennings, who wrote the foreword to a 1998 book titled, "Queering Elementary Education." The book he endorsed was a collection of essays by different authors who supported teaching young children about homosexuality.

Jennings held the position of the "Safe Schools Czar" for the Obama Administration until his resignation on May 23, 2011. During his 14 year tenure at GLSEN, Mr. Jennings touted his homosexual activism and increased the number of public school-based and student-led pro-homosexual clubs, such as Gay-Straight Alliances from 50 to 4300.[17]

HIV/AIDS Education's inaccurate curriculum ignores the fact that male-to-male sexual contact is and has always been the most common cause of HIV transmission. Rather, it stresses that 75% of the disease's transmission is through heterosexual contact, as if some demographic trend in Africa is relevant to the health of American students. The textbooks and materials downplay all risk involved, saying that if you just use condoms you will be okay. Gay rights groups are invited on school campuses to supposedly educate children about problems with bigotry and hate crimes, but end up recounting graphic first-person accounts of their own sexual activities.

Unfortunately, just opting your child out of the sex education portion of health class won't be enough to

---

[17] David Fiorazo, "Eradicate: Blotting Out God In America" (Abbotsford, WI: Life Sentence Publishing), 2012.

protect him or her from this kind of traumatizing information. The ten-week HIV/AIDS course integrates sex education into all aspects of school, including history, music, and literature. Special assemblies are held throughout the year, featuring homosexual activist groups and those sponsored by Planned Parenthood. Explicit questionnaires written as assignments in sex education classes are passed around to other students to fill out. Discussions about homosexuality, condoms, and rape in all classes have been couched in terms of "relevancy" to whatever subject is being presented. Since gay rights are now considered a civil liberties issue, it is openly debated in most classes as well.

Sex education courses promote promiscuity among minors, who legally cannot even give consent to sexual activity. The attitudes of youth today reflect that they believe any behavior between consenting individuals is okay, as long as you don't get sick or pregnant. Gallup's National Values and Beliefs Survey of 2007 found that 75% of 18-34 year-olds see the homosexual lifestyle as an acceptable alternative, compared to just 45% of people 55+ years of age. With the majority of children being indoctrinated into a liberal worldview by the public schools, along with the help of the media and the reinforcement of their peer group, traditional family values are steadily disappearing in America. Marriage is the foundation of the family, and a healthy family is the foundation to a strong society.

Math

The only subject where Secular Humanism doesn't reign supreme is Math, but even this is changing to square with moral relativism these days. If you can give a good enough reason for the answer you came up with, the teacher can grade you according to how he or she felt about your "logic". As little as 20% of an assignment's grade now depends on a mathematically correct answer.[18] The other percentages are subjective grades based on how effectively the student restated the problem, and his/her reasoning and written summary of how he/she came to a solution. Points are even being given based on how the students feel about a particular problem.

It is easy to see that a student who never gives the correct answer to a math fact can do very well in

---

[18] Steven Baldwin & Karen Holgate, "From Crayons To Condoms: The Ugly Truth About America's Public Schools" (Washington, D.C.: WND Books), 2008.

class, while a student who computes the correct answer can receive an "F". Kids who cannot add, subtract, multiply, or divide, but can talk their way out of a paper bag are rewarded, while those that actually studied hard to learn concepts are failed. When children are graded on their feelings in an objective subject like math, it teaches them that feelings and experience trump truth, reasoning, and logic. They are also being taught to produce the socially correct or popular answer, instead of the right answer based on hard facts. When even arithmetic facts and figures become murky, watered down, and fluid, so does the concept of absolute truth.

    The public school system and its administrators have a very specific and troubling plan for how to educate your child. Each subject taught rests on the foundation of Secular Humanism and each furthers, either directly or indirectly, an anti-God agenda. The outcome is students' rejection of family values, preoccupation with death, belief in eugenics, self-destructive behavior, and hatred towards others. Far from being religiously neutral, public education is a government-run system of humanist indoctrination that is hostile to biblical truth and has contributed significantly to the decline of Christianity in our nation.

Bucking The System

Chapter 3: A History of Public Education in America

For the first time, because of the Common Core Standards, K-12 education is being debated on the national stage. Parents and teachers alike are expressing outrage at this curriculum, with its convoluted math concepts and harmful teaching methods detrimental to children's development. Frustrated mothers, fathers, and grandparents all over the country are seeking change at the local and state level, with little results. Educators are leaving the profession in droves, and parents are beginning to pull their kids out of public schools to have them taught at home or at private schools.

On the surface, Common Core appears to be innocuous. In its most basic description, the Common Core State Standards Initiative is a set of national standards for English and Mathematics, supposedly written and copyrighted by the National Governor's Association (NGA) and the Council of Chief State School Officers (CCSSO). Common Core proponents say the Standards were led by a collaboration of states, but both the NGA and CCSSO are Washington, D.C.-based trade associations with no legislative grant of authority from the states to write national school standards. These groups provided a cover for the real drafters of Common Core, Achieve, Inc., a non-profit group in D.C. which consists of advocates for progressive, liberal values.

Backed and primarily funded by the Bill and Melinda Gates Foundation, these "rigorous" standards were adopted sight unseen by 46 states in exchange for Race to the Top grant money (included in President Obama's 2009 Stimulus Bill), and a waiver from No Child Left Behind. The Stimulus Bill allocated $4.35 billion to the U.S. Department of Education to use however it wanted. Most states were reeling from the dismal results of No Child Left Behind, signed into law by George W. Bush, and eager for a change. The standards promised more effective teaching methods, and an opportunity for American children to be able to compete globally with their peers in other countries who consistently scored higher in every major subject.

States adopted the standards during the time of a national recession when states were desperate for money. Applications were sent in November 2009, with a deadline for completion of January 2010. Most state legislatures were in recess during this time period, so governors and state superintendents of education made decisions without consulting their legislatures. In June 2010, the standards were released and states then only had two months to have their school boards sign off on them. Once a state adopted the standards, they could not change them; they were only allowed to add up to 15% of new content in any one area.

Secretary of Education Arne Duncan created the Race To The Top competition, which has been renamed "Race To Nowhere". He was the Superintendent of Chicago Public Schools before being promoted as Secretary of Education by President Obama. Duncan believed that education is the civil rights movement of our day, the only sure way out of poverty and of creating a more just and equal society. In a speech he gave to the Governors Education Symposium held in Cary, NC on June 14, 2009, he stated "What we have is a perfect storm for reform... There has never been this much money [from the Gates Foundation and 2009 Recovery Act] on the table, and there may never be again."[19]

It is important to understand that standards drive and dictate what should be taught in the

---

[19] http://stopcommoncorenc.org/common-core-student-data-tracking-nc-beginnings/

classroom; the curriculum just adds the details. Two testing consortia, Partnership for Assessment of Readiness for College and Careers (PARCC) and Smarter Balanced Assessment Consortia (SBAC), admitted in their applications for grants that they would use federal money to develop curricula methods. The natural result of this scheme was a national curriculum, which is unconstitutional. The 10th Amendment of the U.S. Constitution clearly leaves educational policy up to the individual states.

PARCC tests are administered by Pearson Education, the biggest player in the standardized-testing industry. Pearson also has the contract for the National Assessment of Educational Progress, known as the "Nation's Report Card", and handles the writing portion of the Scholastic Aptitude Test (SAT). Several Islamic countries, such as Saudi Arabia and Libya, own stock in Pearson, along with the Council on American-Islamic Relations and the Muslim Brotherhood. SBAC tests were designed by Linda Darling-Hammond, a radical Stanford professor who partnered with Bill Ayers on some of his education projects. Bill Ayers is best known as the founder of Weather Underground Organization (WUO), a group associated with other international communist guerrilla and terrorist groups, including the Vietcong. Its objective was the furtherance of Soviet foreign policy and the defeat of the U.S. in Vietnam in the 1960s and 70s. The WUO was responsible for roughly 72 bombings, including the United States Capitol, The Pentagon, the United States Department of State, and numerous other targets.

Many people argue that the PARCC and SBAC tests are not needed. National tests have already compared students' progress state to state for years. Less than 2% of students even move to different states according to the U.S. Census Bureau.[20] No correlation has even been found between centralized education and higher performance academically across other nations.

The word "standards" gets an approving nod from the public (and from most educators) because it means "performance that meets a standard." However, the word also means "like everybody else," and standardizing minds is exactly what the Standards try to do. Common Core Standards fans sell the first meaning; the Standards deliver the second meaning.

---

[20] NoToCommonCore. (2012, Nov. 12). Part 1 of 5 Stop the Common Core [Video file]. Retrieved from https://www.youtube.com/watch?v=coRNJluF204

Bucking The System

Standardized minds are about as far out of sync with deep-seated American values as it is possible to get. Nicholas Tampio, Assistant Professor of Political Science at Fordham University, said that the Standards emphasize rote learning and uniformity over creativity, and fail to recognize differences in learning styles.

In response to the standards, the libertarian Cato Institute claimed that "it is not the least bit paranoid to say the federal government wants a national curriculum." Some conservatives have assailed the program as a federal "top-down" takeover of state and local education systems. Diane Ravitch, former U.S. Assistant Secretary of Education and education historian, wrote in her 2013 book *Reign of Error* that the Common Core Standards have never been field-tested and that no one knows whether they will improve education.

According to Common Core Standards, Algebra I is now taught in 9th grade, rather than 8th, which means it will be difficult for students to take Calculus in High School, a requirement for entrance to most higher level universities. Geometry will be taught by an experimental method never used successfully anywhere in the world. Dr. James Milgram, a Stanford University Math Professor, was the only Mathematics content specialist on the 30-person Common Core validation committee, but found the standards to be inadequate. Milgram concluded that by 8th grade, students would be about two grades lower in Math than the highest achieving countries. He described the Common Core standards as "in large measure a political document that, in spite of a number of real strengths, is written at a very low level and does not adequately reflect our current understanding of why the math programs in the high achieving countries give dramatically better results."[21]

University of Arkansas professor Sandra Stotsky was the only English Language Arts (ELA) content specialist on the Common Core validation committee, and refused to sign off on the ELA standards. Testifying before various state legislatures against the Core, she said that they aren't strong enough to prepare students for college. She described the ELA standards as an empty skill set, with no accumulation of literary knowledge. She stated students will be at a 7th grade reading level as seniors in high school, due to the de-emphasis on reading classic literature in favor of non-

---

[21] HSLDA. (2014, Mar. 31). Building the Machine- The Common Core Documentary [Video file]. Retrieved from https://www.youtube.com/watch?v=zjxBClx01jc

fiction, informational texts such as government documents, technical manuals, and even brochures and menus. The philosophy behind this practice is that students shouldn't waste time studying something that won't give them practical assistance in their future jobs.

With this end in mind, Common Core adopts a bottom-line, pragmatic approach to education. The heart of its philosophy is that it is a waste of resources to "over-educate" people. Proponents of Common Core Standards believe the basic goal of K-12 schools is to provide everyone with a modest skill set, and after that people can specialize in college. Their reasoning is truck-drivers do not need to know how to read Huckleberry Finn, physicians have no use for the humanities, and only those destined to major in literature need to worry about Ulysses. Rather than explore the creativity of man, the great lessons of life, tragedy, love, good and evil, and the rich textures of history that underlie great works of fiction, Common Core reduces reading to a servile activity.

The U.S. Dept. of Education is pressuring states to share the data they have collected on students from Pre-K through 12th grade under the Standard's policy. Data mining centers have been built to store and house 400 data points on each child over the 12-13 years they are enrolled in public school. Some of this data includes disciplinary records, health history, family income range, religious affiliation, and parents' political affiliation. Once the Department of Education receives this data, they can then share it with the Department of Labor. The reasoning for this, they say, is to ensure a work force ready population to be able to compete in a global marketplace.

The early rush to adopt Common Core has been displaced by sober second looks and widespread regrets. Of the 45 states that adopted the standards, 4 have repealed them and a dozen others are currently pursuing legislation that could lead to a repeal. Others have opted out of the testing consortia associated with Common Core, but have decided to retain the standards themselves. In short, these standards have failed to deliver what they promised.

Though Common Core is highly destructive to children's learning and development, with methods that smack of Communism, it is only the latest in a series of education reforms throughout the years. Parents hoping to ride out this most recent "reform", or who live in states that have repealed Common Core, need to be aware that the Standards are really just a symptom of a much larger problem. Each change in curricula adds a deeper layer to the already faulty model, which has created debris from all the cultural, social, and moral destruction in our society.

Government-controlled education by definition is a socialist system. The National Education Association has been run by socialists, intending to teach children an atheistic worldview, for almost a century now. Communists have been increasingly influencing the United States with their agenda for nearly 200 years. To find the source of decay in the American education system, we need to go back more than 180 years ago, to 1825.

That year, Robert Owen established the first communist colony in America in New Harmony, Indiana. "Utopian socialist" economic thought such as Owen's grew out of widespread poverty in Britain in the aftermath of the Napoleonic Wars. Communism as an economic and political philosophy was actually created by Owen, not Karl Marx or Vladimir Lenin.[22] He believed that the cause of all of the world's problems was a free enterprise system which fostered selfish desires to compete with others. He believed that

---

[22] Samuel Blumenfeld and Alex Newman, "Crimes of the Educators" (WND Books: Washington, D.C.), 2014.

infants could be molded to have whatever character society wants him or her to have, and that no one is born depraved or evil as religion taught. He desired to reform the world by getting rid of religion, and hoped to turn out rational, cooperative human beings, devoid of selfishness, religious "superstition", and all of the other traits found in men produced by a capitalist system. When his commune in New Harmony failed, Owen decided that a government system of secular education would be the means through which a socialist society could be created.

Robert Owen's son, Robert Dale Owen, helped organize the Workingmen's Party as a front for their socialist ideas, published a radical weekly paper called the *Free Enquirer*, and lectured widely on socialism and national education. At first, Owenites' anti-biblical views turned so many people off that they needed to develop a less obvious strategy. They began forming public opinion subtly by telling Protestants their religious society would be compromised by the increasing immigration of Catholics to the country. Owenites also got men elected to the legislatures that favored education by the state at the public's expense. One such man was Horace Mann, credited by educational historians as the "Father of the Common School Movement".

Mann, a Harvard Unitarian, served in the Massachusetts State Legislature from 1827 to 1837 before being appointed secretary of the newly created state board of education. A member of the Whig Party devoted to promoting speedy modernization, Mann's theme of his oration at Brown University was "The Progressive Character of the Human Race." In 1838, he founded and edited *The Common School Journal.* In this publication, Mann stated his main principles for education were that it should be paid for, controlled, and sustained by an interested public, and that it would be best provided in schools that embrace children from a variety of backgrounds. He supported the notion that this education must be non-sectarian (secular) and should be provided by well-trained, professional teachers.

In 1843, Horace Mann traveled to Germany to investigate how their educational process worked. Upon his return to the United States, he lobbied heavily to have the "Prussian model" adopted. This type of education involved centralized, compulsory, state-funded schools. Prussia's educational system was deliberately designed to produce mediocre intellects, to hamstring the inner life, to deny students appreciable leadership skills, and to ensure docile and incomplete citizens – all in order to render the populace "manageable."[23] Mann's efforts were bankrolled by men of wealth, including the Peabody family, who believed the current literacy rates encouraged more entrepreneurial exuberance than the social system could bear.[24] He was promised Daniel Webster's seat in Congress if he could convince states to adopt the model.

    Arguing that universal public education was the best way to turn the nation's unruly children into disciplined, judicious republican citizens, Mann persuaded his fellow modernizers to legislate tax-supported elementary public schools in their states. 9 years after Mann's visit to Germany, Governor Edward Everett of Massachusetts instituted a mandatory education policy based on the Prussian system, even though the literacy rate in that state was 96% at the time. New York soon set up the same method in 12 different schools on a trial basis. Most

---

[23] John Taylor Gatto, "Weapons of Mass Instruction" (British Columbia, Canada: New Society Publishers), 2009.
[24] Meeting Minutes, Appleton Papers Collection, Massachusetts Historical Society, June 9, 1834.

northern states followed suit, adopting one version or another of the system Mann established in Massachusetts.

Mann worked to create a statewide system of professional teachers, based on the Prussian model of "common schools," which appeared to foster the belief that everyone was entitled to the same content in education. However, Prussia's main purpose of state schooling was not intellectual training, but the conditioning of children to 'obedience, subordination and collective life.' [25] Mann claimed that by bringing children of all classes together, they could have a common learning experience. This would also give the less fortunate, he said, an opportunity to advance in social status.

Compulsory education was thus sold as the equalizer of the conditions of men. The reality is that social class distinctions in America during this time were relatively fluid, since merit in free-market economies produces its own rewards. The country as a whole was not just book-literate, but proficient in

---

[25] John Taylor Gatto, "The Underground History of American Education: A School Teacher's Intimate Investigation Into the Problem of Modern Schooling" (New York, NY: Odysseus Group), 2000.

writing, argumentation, and public speaking, things which had actually been a crime to teach ordinary people under British colonial rule.[26]

Mann also suggested that by having common schools, it would help those students who did not have what he considered appropriate discipline in the home. He wanted to instill "values" such as obedience to authority, promptness in attendance, and organizing time according to bell ringing, believing it would help students prepare for future employment. Mann faced some resistance from parents who did not want to give up moral education to teachers and bureaucrats, however.

In carrying out his work, Mann met with bitter opposition by some Boston schoolmasters who strongly disapproved of his pedagogical ideas (theory and practice of education primarily focused on social skills and cultural norms), and by various religious leaders, who contended against the exclusion of all sectarian instruction from the schools. Early education, even under state control in Massachusetts, had a clear religious intent. An education in reading and religion

---

[26] John Taylor Gatto, "Weapons of Mass Instruction", (British Columbia, Canada: New Society Publishers), 2009.

was required for children by the Massachusetts School Law of 1642. In 1647 the Massachusetts Bay Colony enacted the Old Deluder Satan Law, requiring any township of at least 100 households to establish a grammar school teaching the classical languages as a preparation for university.[27] According to Puritan beliefs, Satan would most definitely try to keep people from understanding the Scriptures, therefore it was deemed that all children be taught how to read.

Up until the introduction of Horace Mann's common school, the school system in America remained largely private and unorganized. Public schools were always under local control, with no federal role, and little state role. Teaching included books such as *The New England Primer*, which taught the alphabet using scriptural references. The *Primer* included additional material that made it widely popular in colonial schools, until it was supplanted by Noah Webster's *Blue Back Speller*. Most schooling was done in one room school houses by teaching students of various ages and abilities together using an education method known as "mutual instruction" or the "Bell-Lancaster method",

---

[27] Stephen V. Monsma and J. Christopher Soper, "The Challenge of Pluralism: Church and State in Five Democracies" (Lanham, MD: Rowman & Littlefield Publishers), 2008.

after British educators Dr. Andrew Bell and Joseph Lancaster. The method was based on the more apt pupils being used as helpers to the teacher, passing on the information they had learned to other students.

One technique Mann learned in Prussia and first introduced in Massachusetts in 1848 was age grading- students were assigned by age to different grades and progressed through them, regardless of differences of aptitude, together with the lecture method used in European universities, which treated students more as passive recipients of instruction than as active participants in instructing one another. Age grading was done to prevent the prospective unity of the peasants and proletarians in Prussia. Dividing children by grades, along with constant rankings on tests, would make it unlikely that these individuals, separated in childhood, would ever re-integrate into a whole to challenge the government. The Prussian system was useful in creating not only a harmless electorate and a servile labor force, but also a virtual herd of mindless consumers.[28]

---

[28] John Taylor Gatto, "Weapons of Mass Instruction" (British Columbia, Canada: New Society Publishers), 2009.

For nearly 30 years, 80% of the public resisted this new law in Massachusetts of compulsory schooling; in 1880, it took the militia to persuade the parents of Barnstable, Cape Cod, to give up their children to the system.[29] Horace Mann would later write in his 1867 book *Lectures and Annual Reports on Education*, "We who are engaged in the sacred cause of education are entitled to look upon all parents as having given hostages to our cause." By 1900, 34 states had compulsory schooling laws, 4 of which were in the South. 30 states with compulsory schooling laws required attendance until age 14 (or higher).[30] As a result, by 1910, 72 percent of American children attended public school. In 1918, every state required students to complete elementary school.

Professor Arthur Calhoun's *Social History of the Family* was written a year later, informing the academic world that big changes were being made to the idea of family. He wrote that the fondest wish of utopian thinkers was coming true: children were passing from blood families "into the custody of

---

[29] Sheldon Richman, "Separating School and State: How to Liberate America's Families" (Fairfax, VA: The Future of Freedom Foundation), 2013.

[30] http://www.heinz.cmu.edu/research/372full.pdf

community experts." In time, the dream of Charles Darwin and Sir Francis Galton would become a reality through the agency of public education, designed to check the mating of the unfit.[31] Sir Francis Galton, Darwin's half-cousin, was the founder of the eugenics movement, which is rooted in selective breeding for positive traits and elimination of negative ones. These "undesirable" traits were concentrated in poor, uneducated, and minority populations.

Edward L. Thorndike, America's leading educational psychologist in the early 20th century, also espoused the principles of eugenics. He devised a new way of learning based on conditioning techniques used in animal training. Thorndike taught the principles of eugenics in his books on teacher training, stating in his 1929 book *Elementary Principles of Education*, "Education, then, cannot improve the racial stock by the direct means of biological hereditary, but it may do so, indirectly, by means of social inheritance." Thorndike advocated that there is no hope of improvement for people who start out with defective genes, therefore they should be trained with a "realistic and industrial

---

[31] John Taylor Gatto, "Weapons of Mass Instruction" (British Columbia, Canada: New Society Publishers), 2009.

curriculum." He is credited, along with John Dewey, as one of the great formative influences of twentieth-century educational theory.[32]

Around the same time, President of the Rockefeller Foundation, Max Muller, announced a comprehensive national program to allow "the control of human behavior". In Muller's mind, planned breeding of human beings was the key to paradise. He wrote the *Geneticists Manifesto*, which included the most basic level of institutional management, the separation of smart kids from "stupid" ones in schools. This separation of children into different intellectual level classrooms, he reasoned, would keep the genetic pool pure. "The perfect organization of the hive with the anthill", H.H. Goddard (for whom The Goddard School is named), Chairman for the Psychology Department at Princeton University, called government schooling approvingly in his 1920 book *Human Efficiency*. "Standardized testing will cause the lower classes to confront their biological inferiority and reproduction will be discouraged among them."

---

[32] Lawrence A. Cremin, "A History of Teachers College" (New York, NY: Columbia University Press), 1954.

Max Muller, an Eastern European geneticist, inspired John D. Rockefeller to invest heavily in the control of human evolution. Rockefeller himself once said, "I don't want a nation of thinkers; I want a nation of workers." Spending more on forced schooling than even the government between 1896 and 1920, Rockefeller hoped this system would produce a group of people who would be trained to follow orders without question and be content to work in mass production. From Rockefeller's General Education Board's document titled *Occasional Letter Number One*, we get a clear picture of what its intended mission was: "In our dreams... people yield themselves with perfect docility to our molding hands. The present educational conventions [of intellect and moral education] fade from our minds, and unhampered by tradition we work our own good will upon a grateful and responsive folk... The task we set before ourselves is very simple; we will organize children... and teach them to do in a perfect way the things their fathers and mothers are doing in an imperfect way."

Rockefeller greatly admired and financially supported the leading educational theorist of that time, John Dewey, called the Father of Modern Education. When Dewey opened The Lincoln School in 1916, the experimental school for Teachers College, Rockefeller donated $3 million to it. Dewey, a long time member of the American Federation of Teachers and college professor, was a "progressive philosopher" and atheist who wanted to transform America into a secular and socialist country. His vision was for the government to take over all education via government schools. He is considered the epitome of liberalism by many historians, sometimes even portrayed as "dangerously radical".

Dewey insisted that education and schooling are instrumental in creating social change and reform. He notes that "education is a regulation of the process of coming to share in the social consciousness; and that the adjustment of individual activity on the basis of this social consciousness is the only sure method of social reconstruction."[33] A follower of Karl Marx, he hailed Marxism as "one of the greatest modern syntheses of humane values". Dewey claimed capitalism imposed a restriction on freedom, and that "socialized industry and finance" would be the means by which people would reach their full potential.

---

[33] John Dewey, "My Pedagogic Creed 1897" (Reprinted by Scholar's Choice: Rochester, NY), 2015.

Karl Marx, in his 1848 book *Communist Manifesto*, describes the 10 steps necessary to destroying a free enterprise system and replacing it with a system of unlimited government power in order to transform a country into a communist socialist state. Free education for all children in public schools is listed as the 10th step. He wrote, "We must abolish the families. We must destroy the most hallowed of relations. We must replace home education with social." Joseph Stalin effectively applied Marx's ideas when he succeeded in transforming Russia into the communist socialist state known as the U.S.S.R. Stalin knew the power of education as a propaganda tool. In just one generation, he converted hordes of the deeply religious Russian people into followers of atheistic Marxism.[34]

Just like in the Soviet Union, the modern American public education system was deliberately designed by John Dewey to separate children from their parents in order to subject them to secular humanist indoctrination. The only difference is that in the United States, it has been done in a more gradual way over the

---

[34] https://answersingenesis.org/culture/gone-in-only-one-generation/

last century. That's exactly the way Dewey planned it. He once stated, "Change must come gradually. To force it unduly would compromise its final success by favoring a violent reaction."[35]

Dewey plotted a long-range, comprehensive strategy that would reorganize primary education to serve the needs of socialization. First, he reduced the emphasis on reading and began implementing social studies programs in curricula. He did away with the traditional intensive phonics method of reading, and imposed a look-say, sight, or whole-word method, so that children do not know how to de-code words and blend sounds together anymore. When the method, originally developed by Reverend Thomas H. Gallaudet for use with deaf and mute children, was first tried with children of normal hearing in Boston in the 1830's, the results were so horrendous that a group of schoolmasters got rid of it and brought back Noah Webster's *Blue Back Speller*.

A colleague of Dewey's, Psychologist James McKeen Cattell, believed that since adults read words as whole units, children should be taught to read total

---

[35] http://www.slblf.com/uploads/2/4/6/5/24650255/181591329-john-dewey-s-plan-to-dumb-down-america-the-primary-education-fetich-forum-1898.pdf

word pictures from the very beginning. What he failed to realize was that an adult reader recognizes the letters in a word so quickly that it seems as if he is reading them as wholes. In order to become proficient in reading, however, a child must first learn the letters and their sounds. What followed was the development of the whole language practice, heavily influenced by Lev Vygotsky, one of the creators of Marxist psychology. Vygotsky espoused ideas about the social nature of learning, along with the Zone of Proximal Development, which entails stressing the importance of collaborations through which students can transcend their own individual limitations.[36] This approach came out of a devotion to making sure that the socialist state in Russia would continue.

By the 1940s, schools everywhere were setting up remedial reading departments and reading clinics to handle the thousands of children with reading problems. Before World War II, when the whole-word method was adopted, literacy rates in the draft pool were 96%. By the Korean War, only 6 years later, they had dropped to 81%. By the time the Vietnam War was

---

[36] Samuel Blumenfeld and Alex Newman, "Crimes of the Educators" (WND Books: Washington, D.C.), 2014.

over, literacy rates among men had fallen to 73%.[37] What was the reason? Dr. Seuss himself had the answer: "I think killing phonics was one of the greatest causes of illiteracy in the country."

Second, Dewey, along with other members of the Progressive Educators of America and the Council on Foreign Relations, did away with basic arithmetic facts including logic and reason. O.A. Nelson stated in an interview with Young Parents Alert that the members wanted to implement a math that pupils could not apply to life situations once they left school. Nelson was in attendance at a special meeting of the Progressive Education Association on December 28, 1928 in which "New Math" was discussed and formulated. He revealed to the Young Parents Alert education conference on April 28, 1979 that the desire of the Progressive Educators of America was to dumb-down students with these modern math methods, and that the group was really a communist front.

Children began being taught mathematics instead of arithmetic. The difference is that arithmetic deals with quantity; math deals with relationships and

---

[37] John Taylor Gatto, "Weapons of Mass Instruction" (British Columbia, Canada: New Society Publishers), 2009.

uses complex symbols. Children need to memorize arithmetic facts because it gives them mastery of the system, and once they are memorized through drill and practice, with pencil and paper, kids will later be able to use calculators and computers with accuracy, spotting errors if they make them, always able to do the calculations on paper if necessary.[38] John Saxon, author of mathematic textbooks used by homeschoolers and private schools with an incremental development and continuous review approach, observed in a 1981 article titled "Supply-side Algebra" in *National Review* magazine: "They have tried to teach advanced concepts and a general overview before the student has learned the basics. In an important sense, these authors are experts neither in mathematics nor in education. They do not know which mathematics topics must be mastered at which level and have no understanding of the capabilities of the average student. Their books are visible proof that they do not know how children learn and assimilate abstractions."

Finally, John Dewey promoted the teaching of Evolution, in order to popularize humanism. He, along

---

[38] Samuel Blumenfeld and Alex Newman, "Crimes of the Educators" (WND Books: Washington, D.C.), 2014.

with other progressives, decided that for the country to become secular and socialist, the young must be less educated and less informed than their parents. This explains why students appear to be performing more poorly academically than each previous generation.

In 1928, Dewey traveled to the former Soviet Union with others from the NEA, and studied the communist education system. The Bolsheviks enjoyed Dewey's books so much they invited him to visit, and *had them translated into Russian.* These are the same books that teachers' colleges and education departments in the United States have used to train a century of public school educators.[39] When Dewey came back, he praised the USSR's development of progressive education ideas and sought to implement them in America.

Five years later, John Dewey co-authored and signed the *Humanist Manifesto*, referring to Humanism as a religious movement that would transcend and replace previous religions. In it, he also refuted the salvation of God through Jesus Christ. He called for the re-education of children away from the

---

[39] David Fiorazo, "Eradicate: Blotting Out God In America" (Abbotsford, WI: Life Sentence Publishing), 2012.

traditional values of their parents and for the redistribution of wealth. "*You can't make socialists out of individualists. Children who know how to think for themselves spoil the harmony of the collective society, which is coming, where everyone is interdependent.*" It was a drastic contrast to the early American settlers whose primary goal and desire for their children's education was to be able to read the Bible proficiently and live its principles freely.

Dewey became the first honorary president of the NEA, and in 1936 the association stated one of its reformed goals as "socializing the individual". Around this time, the NEA also announced that it expected "to accomplish by education what dictators in Europe are seeking to do by compulsion and force." Under Dewey's influence, the NEA began advocating multiculturalism, feminism, socialism, and every other philosophy and worldview that is anti-family and anti-American. Author, columnist, and National Radio and TV host, Brannon Howse states that "the National Education Association has had a long love affair with communism."[40] They know that if the family unit is broken down in America, the government will grow

---

[40] http://www.wnd.com/2010/07/184721/

bigger, due in part to the reliance on welfare. Some of the NEA's contemporary goals include the "right to reproductive freedom", government-run healthcare, the implementation of diversity, tolerance, and anti-bullying programs, gun-control, and opposition to English as the official language in America.

Today, the association employs over 550 staff people and has a budget of more than $307 million per fiscal year. It is part of Education International, the global federation of teachers' unions. Though claiming to be "non-partisan", it is a major supporter of liberal organizations and contributes heavily to the Democratic Party, never having endorsed any Republican or third party candidate. The NEA has become the most powerful special interest group in the U.S., using political lobbying to help elect candidates who will further their progressive agenda, instead of using its influence to improve the quality of American education.

The involuntary union dues collected from teachers adds up to around $40 million dollars each year, disbursed to state affiliates and political issue campaigns. School districts' payroll offices deduct the dues from each teacher's paycheck as a lump sum, then transmit them at regular intervals to the local union affiliate, which keeps its share and submits the remainder to the state affiliate, who then keeps its share and submits the remainder to the national affiliate. The following is a partial list of recipients who benefit from NEA funding: Americans United for Separation of Church and State, Gay and Lesbian Alliance Against Defamation (GLADD), Democratic Leadership Council, Center for American Progress, National Council of La Raza, Amnesty International, Women's Voices, NAACP, and GLSEN.

The top lawyer for the NEA, Bob Chanin, warned about protecting collective bargaining at all costs, saying "it is well recognized that if you take away the mechanism of payroll deduction, you won't collect a penny from these people." Retiring in 2009, he gave his good-bye speech at the annual NEA Convention in San Diego saying "the NEA and its affiliates are the nation's leading advocates for public education and the type of liberal, social, and economic agenda that [conservative and right-wing] groups find unacceptable... Despite what some among us would like to believe, it is not because we care about children. And it is not because we have a vision of a great public school for every child. NEA and its affiliates are effective advocates because we have power. And we have power because there are more than 3.2 million people who are willing to pay us hundreds of millions of dollars in dues each year."[41]

The NEA encourages its employees to emulate Saul Alinsky, "The American Organizer", who called for a method of community organizing involving agitating, aggravating, ridiculing, pressuring, and polarizing. They recommend Alinsky's books to teachers such as *Reveille for Radicals*, about the principles and tactics of community organizing, and *Rules for Radicals*, which articulates a socialist strategy for gaining political power to redistribute wealth. What does this have to do with teaching children and improving education? Nothing, except for the teachers' unions to gain more leverage. They claim their political action is best for the children, but sources show the average public employee makes several times more than the average citizen.[42]

The NEA has had a history of fiercely opposing any competition for public schools such as vouchers, tuition tax credits, or parental option plans. The NEA opposes homeschooling as well, unless kids are taught by state-licensed teachers using a "state approved

---

[41] Gunn Productions. (2011, Oct. 18) Indoctrination [Video file] Retrieved from www.indoctrinationmovie.com

[42] David Fiorazo, "Eradicate: Blotting Out God In America" (Abbotsford, WI: Life Sentence Publishing), 2012.

curriculum". They want to bar homeschooled students from participating in any extracurricular activities in public schools, even though their parents pay school taxes.

When Lyndon Johnson was elected president in 1964, liberals and progressives were given the political power to hand the NEA whatever it asked for, and they gifted them access to the U.S. Treasury. Today, children of the poor are educated for free from Kindergarten through 12th grade, and are eligible for preschool Head Start, Perkins Grants, Pell Grants, and student loans for college.

In 1965, President Johnson passed the Elementary and Secondary Education Act (ESEA) as part of his so-called "War on Poverty", the most far-reaching federal legislation affecting education ever passed by Congress. Up until this time, there had been strong opposition and resistance to federal aid for education. Johnson believed this was the way to build a Great Society, incorrectly tying illiteracy to poverty instead of to the whole language reading method. His "Great Society" social reforms included new major spending programs that addressed education as well as medical care, urban problems, and transportation. These massive programs were one of the catalysts that have put America on the path to economic chaos, with spending on social welfare today approaching the trillion dollar mark.

Despite all the federal funding, however, the literacy disaster continued to grow. By 1969, a blue-ribbon Committee on Reading was appointed by the National Academy of Education to examine America's reading problems and offer recommendations on how to solve them. The Committee's 1975 report entitled *Toward a Literate Society* stated, "It is not cynical to suggest that the chief beneficiaries of the Elementary and Secondary Education Act have been members of the school systems- both professional and paraprofessional- for whom new jobs were created." In other words, the children, for whom the ESEA was supposedly designed for, had not benefited from the massive spending by the government on education. To deal with the problem of reading deficiencies, the committee offered a radical suggestion: create a voucher system to help students buy reading instruction. "We believe that an effective national reading effort should bypass the existing education macrostructure," they continued in their report. They also stated that the existence of vested interests in maintaining the status quo impeded improvements in education.

Despite these revelations, in 1979 President Jimmy Carter upgraded education to cabinet level status, creating the United States Department of Education. The USDE is one of the richest government gravy trains in American history, with a current annual budget of over $71 billion dollars. Many outside the Democratic Party viewed its creation as "an unnecessary and illegal federal bureaucratic intrusion into local affairs, funded by taxpayers."[43] Some claim that Carter created the USDE in return for the support he received during his campaign from the teachers' unions. In every presidential election since the USDE's inception, the National Education Association has endorsed or supported Democratic candidates.

In 1982, President Reagan's Secretary of Education ordered another survey of America's failing education system. An 18-member National Commission on Excellence in Education was created, issuing a report a year later. "The educational foundations of our society are presently being eroded by

---

[43] David Fiorazo, "Eradicate: Blotting Out God In America" (Abbotsford, WI: Life Sentence Publishing), 2012.

a rising tide of mediocrity that threatens our very future as a nation and a people," the report exclaimed. Titled *A Nation at Risk: The Imperative for Education Reform*, it went on to say "If an unfriendly foreign power had attempted to impose on America the mediocre educational performance that exists today, we might well have viewed it as an act of war."

The systemic change needed to address these problems never happened, and schools continued to rely on faulty reading and math methods. Instead, Achieve Inc. was formed in 1996 at the Educational Summit in New York as a collaboration of governors, corporate leaders, and the National Center on Education and the Economy to create benchmark education standards and assessments. These were designed to force schools to follow Goals 2000, which is based on the premise of outcomes-based education that students will reach higher levels of achievement when more is expected of them. The goals outlined were:

- All children in America will start school ready to learn.
- The high school graduation rate will increase to at least 90 percent.

- All students will leave grades 4, 8, and 12 having demonstrated competency over challenging subject matter including English, mathematics, science, foreign languages, civics and government, economics, the arts, history, and geography, and every school in America will ensure that all students learn to use their minds well, so they may be prepared for responsible citizenship, further learning, and productive employment in our nation's modern economy.
- United States students will be first in the world in mathematics and science achievement.
- Every adult American will be literate and will possess the knowledge and skills necessary to compete in a global economy and exercise the rights and responsibilities of citizenship.
- Every school in the United States will be free of drugs, violence, and the unauthorized presence of firearms and alcohol and will offer a disciplined environment conducive to learning.
- The nation's teaching force will have access to programs for the continued improvement of their professional skills and the opportunity to acquire the knowledge and skills needed to

> instruct and prepare all American students for the next century.
> - Every school will promote partnerships that will increase parental involvement and participation in promoting the social, emotional, and academic growth of children.[44]

None of these eight educational goals were actually attained by the year 2000 as was originally intended.

In 2002 No Child Left Behind (NCLB) was passed by a bipartisan coalition in Congress, marking a new direction. In exchange for more federal aid, individual states were required to develop its own standards and assessments in basic skills at select grade levels. The Act did not assert a national achievement standard. NCLB expanded the federal role in public education through further emphasis on annual testing, annual academic progress, report cards, and teacher qualifications, as well as significant changes in funding.

Schools received a grade based on their students' test scores, called their AYP (Adequate Yearly Progress) Number, and either got Title I funding removed or were marked as "needing improvement". Title I is a provision of the ESEA, to distribute funding

---

[44] https://en.wikipedia.org/wiki/Goals_2000

to schools and school districts with a high percentage of students from low-income families. Title I also helps children from families that have migrated to the United States and youth from intervention programs who are neglected or at risk of abuse. In addition, Title I appropriates money to the education system for prevention of dropouts and the improvement of schools. In its original conception, Title I was designed by President Johnson to close the skill gap in reading, writing and mathematics between children from low-income households who attend urban or rural school systems, and children from the middle-class who attend suburban school systems.

The unfortunate result was that in order not to lose this funding under No Child Left Behind, principals either dumbed down the curriculum or instructed each teacher to "teach to the test". Critics argue that the focus on standardized testing (all students in a state taking the same test under the same conditions) encourages teachers to teach a narrow subset of skills that the school believes increases test performance, rather than achieve in-depth understanding of the overall curriculum. For example, a teacher who knows that all questions on a math test are simple addition problems might not invest any class time on the practical applications of addition, to leave more time for the material which the test assesses. By 2012 most states were given waivers from NCLB in exchange for adopting the Common Core State Standards Initiative, because the original goal that 100% of students be deemed "proficient" by 2014 had proven unrealistic.

While Common Core is certainly rotten from the inside out, the system has been in decay since the mid-19th century. The current debate about whether we should have a national curriculum is phony- we have already had one for over a century. For all of the educational reforms made over the last 160 years, the most we have to show for it today is a government controlled education monopoly. Colin Gunn, producer and director of the documentary *IndoctriNation*, stated "We are now facing all these problems in America- high taxation, welfare dependency, government debt- and as Christians and conservatives we have to see we can't solve those problems until we solve the public schooling problem."[45]

---

[45] http://www.christianpost.com/news/documentary-challenging-anti-christian-indoctrination-in-public-schools-wins-award-70935/

Under this bureaucratic education system, children's critical thinking is discouraged and their imaginations are crippled. Because of union contracts, most teachers get paid about the same regardless of performance, leaving little incentive to improve. Tenure makes it nearly impossible for teachers to be fired for incompetence. National graduation rates and achievement scores are flat, while spending on education has increased more than 100% since 1971.

Over the past century and a half of the American education system, humanists and socialists have sought to indoctrinate youth with their philosophies, while deliberately dumbing down curriculum. The outcome has been abysmal academic results and moral decline in all sectors of society. We don't need more reforms; we need to jettison the model completely.

Bucking The System

Chapter 4: Biblical Principles for Education

John Taylor Gatto is the three-time winner of the New York City Teacher of the Year Award and was named as 1991 New York State Teacher of the Year. He wrote about his teaching experience in *Weapons of Mass Instruction: A Schoolteacher's Journey through the Dark World of Compulsory Schooling*. Summing up his thoughts in an interview for the documentary film *IndoctriNation*, he exclaimed "Is there an idea more radical in the history of the human race than turning your children over to complete strangers, who you know nothing about, and having those strangers work on your child's mind- out of your sight- for a period of twelve years? Back in colonial days in America, if you proposed that as an idea, they'd burn you at the stake." Yet today, 85% of Christians send their children to the public schools for their education.[46]

When colonists settled in the United States, they educated by the traditional English methods of family, church, community, and apprenticeship. Family

---

[46] Bruce Shortt, "The Harsh Truth About Public Schools" (Vallecito, CA: Chalcedon), 2004.

and church were the key agents of socialization back then. At first, the rudiments of literacy and arithmetic were taught inside the family, assuming the parents had those skills. Of course, by the mid-19th century, the role of the schools had expanded to such an extent that many of the educational tasks traditionally handled by parents became the responsibility of the schools.

Christian education has a rich tradition of helping to form children's hearts and minds. In that tradition, education brings children to the Word of God. It provides students with a sound foundation of knowledge and sharpens their faculties of reason. It nurtures the child's natural openness to truth and beauty, his moral goodness, and his longing for the infinite. It equips students to understand the laws of nature and to recognize the face of God in their fellow man. Education in this tradition forms men and women capable of discerning and pursuing their path in life and who stand ready to defend truth, their church, their families, and their country. As we have seen in the previous chapters, public education does just the opposite.

The public school system is not designed for a free society. Teachers in the public school, whether they are Christians or not, are still required by the government to use a godless curriculum (and not religiously neutral, remember). They are merely pedagogues, a word dating back to Ancient Rome meaning "slave". The pedagogue was a specialized servant responsible for driving home a curriculum created by the Master who owned him, and made sure the pupil made it to school on time. The principle of citizen oversight has become the great school illusion.[47]

School boards, superintendents, principals, and teachers simply carry out the will of the State. A professionalized pedagogy works in tandem with government to recommit the institution to the service of corporate economy. Any political management, even tyranny, must provide enough labor for ordinary people that revolutionary conditions don't emerge. Institutional schooling is *the* principal employer in the United States. It grants more contracts than even the Department of Defense.[48] Parents and teachers are virtually powerless to create any kind of meaningful change. Teachers and administrators who are

---

[47] John Taylor Gatto, "Weapons of Mass Instruction" (British Columbia, Canada: New Society Publishers), 2009.

[48] Samuel Blumenfeld and Alex Newman, "Crimes of the Educators" (WND Books: Washington, D.C.), 2014.

Christian can really only give vague examples of how to live morally, without mentioning the name of Jesus.

Parental rights essentially do not exist beyond the threshold of the school door. The ruling in the case of Fields v. Palmdale School District stated "once parents make the choice as to which school their children will attend, their fundamental right to control the education of their children is, at the least, substantially diminished." Fathers are commanded to bring their children up in the discipline and instruction of the LORD, with mothers as their primary helpers, and with the support of the church (Ephesians 6:4, Psalm 78:5-8, and Deuteronomy 6:1-7). According to the U.S. First and Ninth Circuit Court of Appeals, in the public schools the state determines what the children will be taught, not the father.

Furthermore, when parents send their children to government schools, they are communicating to their children that the school personnel are the authority that child should listen to, learn from, believe, and become like, instead of themselves. Jesus said in Luke 6:40, "A pupil is not above his teacher; but everyone, after he has been fully trained, will be like his teacher." The one who holds the child's heart will be the one discipling him. Do we want our children's hearts and loyalty given to the state, or to us as their parents and, ultimately, God?

Unfortunately, we end up giving away much of our God-given influence to complete strangers because it is ingrained in our minds that we are not qualified to educate our own children. Hillary Clinton's 1996 book *It Takes a Village: And Other Lessons Children Teach Us* minimizes traditional family and declares that organizations outside the family can meet children's needs. Sadly, even the church has bought this lie hook, line, and sinker. Christian parents outsource the education of their children to the government, convinced that the "professionals" know better than they do how to instruct kids in math, science, reading, and writing.

Nothing could be further from the truth! Scripture contains many principles concerning parents' responsibility to educate their children. People assume that because the Bible doesn't mention "public school", it is silent on the issue. The Bible doesn't mention "credit cards" either, but Scripture is full of warnings not to borrow money. Likewise, the Bible is full of warnings not to associate with idol worshipers or be conformed to this world. Jeremiah 10:2 clearly says, "Thus says the LORD: 'Do not learn the ways of the heathen.'" Why would we, then, willingly hand our children over to be taught by them?

Psalm 1:3 says, "How blessed is the man who does not walk in the counsel of the wicked, nor stand in the path of sinners, nor sit in the seat of scoffers! But his delight is in the law of the Lord, and in His law he meditates day and night. He will be like a tree firmly planted by streams of water, which yields its fruit in its season and its leaf does not wither; and in whatever he does, he prospers." When our kids sit under the teaching, or counsel, of the godly, they will reap blessings. Education is not simply about accumulating facts and figures; it is about wisdom. Our children become wise when they walk with those who know and fear the Lord.

Proverbs 9:10 states, "The fear of the LORD is the beginning of wisdom, and the knowledge of the Holy One is understanding." Government schools lack the fear of the LORD; therefore they cannot properly transmit wisdom, knowledge, and understanding. If our kids spend the majority of their decisive years in an environment that does not teach respect for God, they arguably cannot learn true knowledge. At best, they are learning man's wisdom, which isn't really wisdom at all. Economic Historian Gary North states, "[as the parent]

You would be unwise to allocate that much of his [your child's] time to the Kingdom of Man... The child is drawn out into service, the question is: whom will he serve? God's interests, or man's?"[49]

1 Corinthians 1:19-20 says there is no room for worldly wisdom that raises itself up against the knowledge of God. "For it is written, 'I WILL DESTROY THE WISDOM OF THE WISE, AND THE CLEVERNESS OF THE CLEVER I WILL SET ASIDE.' Where is the wise man? Where is the scribe? Where is the debater of this age? Has not God made foolish the wisdom of the world?" Government schools make a mockery of God's Word, relegating it to a mythical collection of stories, instead of regarding it as the source of true wisdom. The public school system intentionally keeps out the necessary elements of the Gospel, such as God as the Creator and Sovereign Judge of the Universe, the Substitutionary Atonement of Jesus Christ and His resurrection, and the call to repent of your sins. Children are taught directly, and indirectly, that there is no need for a Savior or for the Scriptures.

---

[49] Gunn Productions. (2011, Oct. 18) Indoctrination [Video file] Retrieved from www.indoctrinationmovie.com

Without knowledge being predicated on the foundation of Christ, children are susceptible to chasing after the world's ideas and philosophies. Colossians 2:8 warns, "See to it that no one takes you captive through philosophy and empty deception, according to the tradition of men, according to the elementary principles of the world, rather than according to Christ." Taking in secular, humanistic thoughts through various teaching methods in the classroom has the very dangerous potential to lead impressionable children away from the Lord. Being immersed in that kind of godless culture will eventually wear off on our kids, despite all our teaching at home.

2 Corinthians 6:14-15 is clear that as Christian parents, we are forbidden to partner with unbelievers in the education of our children. "Do not be bound together with unbelievers; for what partnership have righteousness and lawlessness, or what fellowship has light with darkness? Or what harmony has Christ with Belial, or what has a believer in common with an unbeliever? Or what agreement has the temple of God with idols? For we are the temple of the living God; just as God said, "I WILL DWELL IN THEM AND WALK AMONG THEM; AND I WILL BE THEIR GOD, AND THEY SHALL BE MY PEOPLE." We tend to

view this scripture in light of a marriage or business partnership, but it also applies to the partnering we do with our child's teachers. These educators' teachings should match up with the Word of God, not espouse humanist ideas.

The Apostle Paul had this to say about teaching a false gospel in Galatians 1:8-9: "But even if we, or an angel from heaven, should preach to you a gospel contrary to what we have preached to you, he is to be accursed! As we have said before, so *I say again now, if any man is preaching to you a gospel contrary to what you received, he is to be accursed!*" (emphasis mine). Our children sit under the teaching of this false gospel, six to seven hours each day, five days a week, 180 days per year, for at least 12 years of their life, during their most impressionable years. The Sunday School instruction they receive once or twice a week is a drop in the bucket to prevent this kind of teaching. Charles Francis Potter, a signatory of the *Humanist Manifesto*, knew this all too well when he wrote, "What can the theistic Sunday-school, meeting for an hour once a week, and teaching only a fraction of the children, do to stem the tide of a five-day program of humanistic teaching?"[50]

The average church's elementary Sunday School program is sorely lacking in the education needed to train up children in the Word. Kids learn the individual stories in the Bible, but there is little to no emphasis on how they all fit together as part of a big picture. Fixed Point Foundation, in their nationwide survey of college students who are members of the Secular Student Alliances or Freethought Societies, found that this lack of connected understanding was one of the most significant reasons that college-age atheists had left Christianity. They "heard plenty of messages encouraging 'social justice,' community involvement, and 'being good,' but they seldom saw the relationship between that message, Jesus Christ, and the Bible."[51] Children are rarely taught in traditional Sunday School how to apply biblical principles to their everyday lives and to take ownership of their sins. Even if they do attend a church with an excellent program, two hours

---

[50] Charles Francis Potter, "Humanism: A New Religion" (New York, NY: Simon and Schuster), 1930.

[51] http://www.theatlantic.com/national/archive/2013/06/listening-to-young-atheists-lessons-for-a-stronger-christianity/276584/

per week isn't enough to counteract all of the secular teaching they receive in public school.

The church is supposed to support parents in their role as primary spiritual influences over their children, not assume this role for them. God holds mothers and fathers accountable first and foremost for the spiritual instruction of the children He has entrusted them with. "Hear, my son, your father's instruction and do not forsake your mother's teaching" (Proverbs 1:8). It is assumed that the father and mother are doing the teaching. No one else is mentioned in Scripture as having that role.

1 Thessalonians 2:11 says, "just as you know how we were exhorting and encouraging and imploring each one of you as a father would his own children…" In this passage, exhorting means "inviting" or "calling near"; encouraging means "consoling" or "comforting"; and imploring means literally "flogging" or "scourging." It is assumed in Scripture that fathers are taking responsibility for drawing their children to themselves for instruction, comfort, and physical discipline. Notice that the verse says, "his own children," not someone else's.

Ephesians 6:4 states, "Fathers, do not provoke your children to anger, but bring them up in the discipline and instruction of the Lord." What kind of counsel does the public school provide on matters like purity or finances? It is a parent's job to bring his children up in the biblical counseling of God, not of the world. Parents must also take responsibility for passing on true providential history to their own children and grandchildren. We should not allow the faithfulness of God in history to be revised, hidden, or concealed in their textbooks or by ungodly teachers. "We will not conceal them from their children, but tell to the generation to come the praises of the LORD, and His strength and His wondrous works that He has done" (Psalm 78:4). Our kids will not hear glory being given to God for much of anything in the public schools.

    The government education system's foundations are built upon the worldview that man controls his own destiny and reigns supreme. This is akin to building a structure on sand, instead of rock, as Jesus said in Matthew 7. Scripture tells us that everyone who hears Christ's words and puts them into practice may be compared to that wise man who built his house on the rock. The house was able to stand firm against the harsh elements, and we will be able to weather the storms of life. Psalm 127:1 says, "Unless the LORD builds the house, they labor in vain who build it." If our families are not built on God's Word, our efforts in raising them are futile.

Now, there are many arguments that Christians make in favor of sending children to public school, mainly that they can be a witness to their peers. There exists a quasi-biblical doctrine which twists "go therefore and make disciples of all the nations" into "let the nations teach your kids." Somehow, we believe that the Great Commission applies to young, impressionable children who have only a rudimentary understanding of theology and biblical principles. A careful examination of this verse tells us that it was an instruction for mature believers, and that the verb "go" can be understood as perpetual, as in "going". Mature disciples, as they go about their day, are supposed to make other disciples. No matter which translation of Matthew 28:19 you read, it says "disciples", *not converts*. There is a big difference in sending fully trained disciples into enemy territory and sending recruits to our enemy's training camp. If we do the latter, we shouldn't be surprised when they come home wearing the enemy's uniform and charging the hill of our home while waving an enemy flag.[52]

The salt and light argument is used as well. Matthew 5:13-16 does not say *go be* salt and light, however, it says we *are* salt and light, and we must be careful as to not lose our saltiness and become useless. A city or light set on a hill is set apart and distinct, so that we may maintain a witness. Children by their very nature are extremely vulnerable to influence and ruination as salt and light. They need to develop deep roots first, formed within the greenhouse of the home, before they're ready to be transplanted out into the world.

A child's saltiness is lost almost immediately when he is thrust into the public school system. He is not capable of rejecting anti-biblical notions on his own, because he has not yet formed critical thinking skills. Ephesians 4:14 says, "... We are no longer to be children, tossed here and there by waves and carried about by every wind of doctrine, by the trickery of men, by craftiness in deceitful scheming." We should wait on sending them out of the "nest" until they're strong, well

---

[52] Voddie Baucham, Jr. , "Family Driven Faith: Doing What It Takes to Raise Sons and Daughters Who Walk With God" (Wheaton, IL: Crossway Books), 2007.

equipped, and established in their faith- otherwise they are very likely to have that faith killed off, to be swayed by strong environmental forces or peers, or to be infected by hazardous ideas.

In his 1897 book *Come Ye Children: A Book for Parents and Teachers on the Christian Training for Children,* Charles Spurgeon wrote "Children in grace have to grow, rising to greater capacity in knowing, being, doing, and feeling, and to greater power from God; therefore above all things they must be FED. They must be WELL fed or instructed, because they are in danger of having their cravings perversely satisfied with error! Youth are susceptible to false doctrine." Children soak up learning like sponges, becoming filled with whatever goes into their minds, and ultimately, their hearts. If we don't feed them continually with the Word, they will have their appetites for knowledge satisfied elsewhere. Sending our kids to public schools where they are immersed in a toxic student culture, and taught moral relativism and a secular humanist worldview, is a recipe for disaster.

It is in our nature to love sin. We have no idea how disgusting sin really is, until God regenerates our hearts and makes us born again. Imagine if God snapped His fingers and changed a pig into a human being in the middle of eating pods. That person would be desperate for someone to clean him. That's what it means to be truly converted. This does not describe the majority of our children, unfortunately, although they are raised in Christian homes and attend weekly church services. Most of them do not yet have the capacity to understand how wretched they are in their sins and the depths of God's judgment which they deserve. How can these very young children be salt and light in the public schools when God has not yet regenerated their hearts and lead them to repentance and faith?

There is the transfer of authority at play here, too. While in school, children are under the authority of their teachers. Teachers and administrators act in loco parentis, Latin for "in the place of a parent". They are granted the legal responsibility to take on some of the functions and responsibilities of the parent while children are on school grounds, acting in the best interests of students as they see fit. Students are expected to obey their teachers and other staff, restricting their freedom to witness to their peers. Sharing their Christian faith is often seen as bullying, for the sake of "tolerance".

Certainly, we can expect that some extraordinary students who manage to find biblical footing despite their educations will have some positive impact on those around them. However, take one or two Christian kids, put them in a classroom with 20 undisciplined children, along with one teacher who doesn't know what Truth is, and have them discuss worldly issues, ignoring God for 30 hours a week. Whose influence will rub off on whom? "Do not be deceived: 'Bad company corrupts good morals'" (1 Corinthians 15:33). Peer pressure and the school's policy against sharing one's faith makes it difficult for even the strongest Christian youth.

Considering the toxic nature of the public school environment, even truly born again children are ill suited for this kind of "missionary" work. A father of seven homeschooled children, who decided to then put his children in public school, came to the conclusion that he had misapplied biblical instruction meant for adult believers to children who shouldn't be expected to function at the same level of spiritual hardiness that God expects from adults: "In not one instance can I say that my kids were able to make a significant salt-and-light impact in their public schools, regardless of how popular they were. The truth is, in every case, their own faith and walk with Christ universally suffered from the experience. The Old Testament is filled with case studies of what happens when God's people surround themselves with a pagan culture; how was it that I expected something different for my kids whose faith was only developing? Simply stated, when I put my kids in public school, I relinquished the greatest influence I have to disciple them, and I delegated that role to the teachers and students of the public school: I chose to have my kids discipled by Humanists."[53]

Over and over again in Scripture, God tells the Israelites to be separate from their pagan neighbors. He wanted them to be "holy unto the Lord". Moses didn't tell God that he thought the exodus was a bad idea, because the Egyptians would lose the positive influence of the Israelites. God called His people (including the children!) *out* of Egypt. Then, after they entered the promised land, He specifically directed them to destroy all the people living there so they would not be corrupted by the idol worshippers' practices. 1 Peter 2:9 also tells us we are a royal priesthood, set apart for God. 2 Corinthians 6:17-18 says, "Therefore, COME OUT FROM THEIR MIDST AND BE SEPARATE," says the Lord. "AND DO NOT TOUCH

---

[53] http://indoctrinationmovie.com/a-fathers-testimony-2/

WHAT IS UNCLEAN; and I will welcome you. "And I will be a father to you, and you shall be sons and daughters to Me," says the Lord Almighty."

Buddhists, Hindus, Jews, Muslims, and other people of various faiths do not send their children to school expecting them to be proselytized, either. Those parents have the right to expect the spiritual development of their child to be under their own control. Children belong to their parents. Christians do not have any right to undermine the upbringing of a child who is not their own, even with the goal of making them believers of the Gospel.

Acts gives us example upon example of houses being converted to Christianity. The parents, usually the father, became disciples first and then led the rest of their household to Christ. In not one instance is a child proselytized against the wishes of the parent, and children are never made the focus of a conversion campaign. Seeking to do so is a direct affront to the institution of the family that God designed. Reaching kids with ideas while they are separated from the authority of their parents is a way in which Christians attempt to take advantage of compulsory education. What they do not realize is that new age utopians are taking the same advantage of the absence of parents-*and getting much better results.*

The proof is in the pudding, as they say. If Christian children are evangelizing other students and leading them to the Lord at a great rate, we would have seen positive results after more than a century. After all, 85% of Christian parents send their kids to public schools in this country. However, the opposite effect has occurred, with disastrous results. The fact is that children have been influenced *away* from Christ, not towards Him. Princeton Theological Seminary Professor A.A. Hodge said in 1887, "I am as sure as I am of Christ's reign that a comprehensive and centralized system of national education, separated from religion, as is now commonly proposed, will prove the most appalling enginery for the propagation of anti-Christian and atheistic unbelief, and of anti-social nihilistic ethics, individual, social and political, which this sin-rent world has ever seen." He was right.

Chapter 5: Discovering a Better Way

Globalism, evolution, whole-language reading methods, fuzzy math, graphic sex education, and moral relativism taught in public schools have led to a steep decline in literacy, preoccupation with death and suicide, and a war against biblical religion and morality. The de-emphasis of the 3 R's (reading, writing, and arithmetic), and the replacement of God's knowledge with man's wisdom in public education has resulted in a pervasive, atheistic worldview in America, even among those who call themselves Christian. This is a dismal assessment of our nation's education system, but there is good news! Parents still have the freedom to educate their children outside this corrupt government system.

Jack A. Chambless, an economics professor at Valencia College, wrote an article making a strong case for homeschooling as the best academic option in America. The following is an excerpt from his article:
For the past 21 years I have taught economics to more than 14,000 college students here in Central Florida. During that time I have made a concerted effort to glean information from my Valencia students as to their educational background preceding their arrival in college. Drawing from a sample size this large

multiplied by two decades multiplied by hundreds of thousands of test answers has put me in a good position to offer the following advice to any reader of this paper with children in Florida's K-12 public schools. Get them out now before you ruin their life.[54]

It starts with believing that you, as the parent, are qualified to educate your child(ren) despite what so-called experts say. After all, no one knows your child better than you do. You know what makes them tick. You can anticipate their needs before they articulate them. You have been there for every milestone, wiped their tears, and encouraged them through difficult tasks.

You have already been teaching them every single day about how the world works, helping them develop character and independence. By example, you have shown them how to love and serve others, how to express themselves, and how to see themselves through God's eyes. You have read them books, taught them how to count, and encouraged them to create works of art using finger paint, watercolors, and crayon scribbling. You have been incredibly influential on

---

[54] Jack A. Chambless, "Is it time to think about home schooling your child?", *Orlando Sentinel*, June 10, 2012.

them during the most crucial years of their development. Why does your role in their education drastically drop off the day they start Kindergarten?

You do not need to be super organized and super patient. Regular, "ordinary moms" who allow an extraordinary God to work through them to do incredible things will suffice. You also don't need to start growing your own vegetables and making your own butter and clothes. And that denim jumper? Not a requirement, either. Those are all preconceived notions you may have had about what it means to be a homeschooling mother. Frankly, I had the same ones. I can tell you it doesn't look anything like what you imagined. It looks like basically whatever you want it to, based on your particular family's needs.

As their parent, you are in the best position to teach your children according to their unique needs, talents, abilities, and interests. True learning takes place when children are free to explore the world around them, not tethered to a chair in one room for six hours. Children are naturally curious, which explains many of the messes in my home! That curiosity does not stop at the school door, but because of the limitations of a classroom's schedule and often a single-use room, this innate feeling becomes stifled over time.

Proper sitting and non-disruptive behavior is favored in school over movement and the messes that often come with being creative. Kids eventually lose the ability to invent, as they now wait for the teacher to tell them what to do and how to do it.

Studies have shown that children whose movements are restricted do not learn as well as when they are free to move around. This may be why we are seeing an explosion in the diagnosis of ADHD, especially in young boys. Boys, by design, are more physical than girls. They need to release pent up energy with physical movements. With the cutting back on recess time and gym classes, this gives them even less opportunity for release. This explains why your sons (and even daughters) become "wild" as soon as they arrive home from school. If they have been concentrating all their efforts on paying attention and not fidgeting in class, they usually sacrifice the ability to control other impulses.

Prior to my son being educating at home, this described his experience in a regular school environment. Despite great teachers and relatively small class sizes, he still struggled academically. I spoke with his teachers, working with them to find solutions, and did my best to implement all the strategies at home that they suggested. In spite of our joint efforts, during one parent/teacher conference I heard the words every parent dreads: "learning disability". He did very well processing and retaining information when we worked one on one at home, though, so I began to think that maybe the only difference was the learning environment.

Like most six-year-old boys, he was very active and energetic, and had difficulty processing information when there was a lot of noise or activity in the background. He also struggled with two-step directions. The over-stimulation from the busyness of the classroom and the sharp transitions between play time and seat work made it hard for him to understand what the teacher wanted him to do. He would sit down and stare at his paper blankly, because he did not process the directions given. He was still thinking about what he and another kid were talking about five minutes ago, or the fun game he had just been playing on the playground.

At home, he can stand instead of sit still to do his math problems, walk around the room while answering questions, and play with cars or Legos while I'm reading to him. Here, if he doesn't understand something he can ask me to explain it again in another way, as many times as it takes. Since he doesn't have to rush through assignments because of the class's schedule, he can take his time and really produce something he will be proud of. If he wants to know more about something, we can go down a rabbit trail discussing it, using Google or YouTube to find more information.

Many people argue that children taught at home are sheltered and cannot deal with the realities of the world, not having been "socialized" in a regular school environment. To the contrary, kids who are homeschooled have *more* opportunities to engage with the world since they are not confined to the 8am to 2:30pm schedule in one location and the demands of homework. Their schedule is flexible, allowing for real world experiences such as volunteering at charitable organizations, going on mission trips, visiting places of business, and seeing their elderly neighbors. They are able to interact with people of all ages, preparing them for how it will be when they are in the workforce, instead of primarily with peers their own age. Grouping them together with children born within the same year only serves to keep them interested in childish things.

Recently, our church hosted a conference for strengthening the family. The speaker brought his wife and the four youngest of their seven children to the seminar. Each child, ranging in age from 13 to 18, spoke about their experiences growing up in a connected family that turned inwardly to one another for worth instead of outwardly. The way that each one carried, expressed, and presented themselves was very impressive. After the conference, I asked their mother if they were homeschooled. She replied that she had been homeschooling for the past 25 years! My suspicions were confirmed.

Home-educated kids can (usually) be spotted a mile away. They are well-spoken, wise beyond their years, and independent, not living according to bells or hall passes. They move fluidly between what appears at times like different child and adult "realms", handling themselves with maturity, yet possessing innocence at the same time. They also seem to be free in the sense that they do not care what peers think about their faith in Jesus, nor are they weighed down with their expectations. These kids don't have weight of the world on them either, having not been immersed in a secular environment for their schooling. Far from being sheltered, they have read great literary works most adults have never read, built homes for the poor in developing countries, organized charitable drives, ministered to people in foreign nations, and built their own businesses from the ground up. Their passion for the Lord, as well as their entrepreneurial spirit, is infectious.

No, kids that are educated at home will not grow up in a bubble, nor should they. We have examined how public school deluges youth with humanist teachings, offering no alternative of a biblical faith or viewpoint. Our children should only be exposed to worldly teachings so that they will be inoculated against them. The idea is to engage our kids in learning about other cultures, religions, and worldviews while they are under our protection.

We should be proactive in engaging our kids in discussing answers from a Christian worldview, so that they will be ready to make a defense to everyone who asks them to give an account for the hope that is in them, yet with gentleness and respect (1 Peter 3:15). As Christian parents, we want to prepare our children to appropriately respond to the world's questions, and often harsh criticisms, about Christianity and biblical teachings. Churches, by and large, are not equipping children with apologetics. It is our job to not only teach them the core beliefs of our faith, but to educate them how to defend those beliefs as well.

We don't want our children to be like those who are always learning and never able to come to the knowledge of the truth (2 Timothy 3:7). As a homeschooling mom, I am not merely educating my children at home. I am also discipling them. I teach God's providential rule over creation and history, as well as addition, subtraction, reading, and spelling. I have the ability to shape my children's worldview according to God's Word, and instruct them in the ways of the Lord, instead of exposing them to the empty pagan philosophies of the world.

Ultimately, a biblical education is the direct application of the Great Commission in our homes. The Great Commission not only includes the preaching of the gospel and baptizing new believers, but also the making of mature believers by teaching them to obey everything Jesus commanded. This is the goal of a truly biblical education. The Great Commission needs to begin with our family, expand to our friends and extended family, our local community, and then to the rest of the world.

Biblical education involves more than just imparting knowledge. It involves the shaping of character through a close, personal relationship between the teacher and his/her student. In this setting, parents can walk beside their children as they expose them to the world and its many issues from a biblical perspective. It allows for mothers and fathers to consistently train their children's character by the application of biblical discipline. Teaching and modeling spiritual disciplines such as prayer, Bible study, scripture memorization, and Christian service can help prepare your children to become mature believers who are ready to serve the Lord.

Loving your kids by living life daily with them, teaching, guiding, and training them has the greatest potential for fostering the strongest possible parent-child relationships, too. As a result of this kind of teaching, parents hold the greatest position of influence over their children's education and discipleship. God intends for it to be this way. In Deuteronomy 6:6-7 we read, "These words, which I am commanding you today, shall be on your heart. You shall teach them diligently to your sons and shall talk of them when you sit in your house and when you walk by the way and when you lie down and when you rise up." Israelite parents taught these truths to their children as they went about their daily lives with them; they did not send their children off to pagans to be taught "the basics".

Joe White, President of Kanakuk Kamps, says the "closest light to their eyes is always the brightest". The people who have the greatest influence over your children are the ones closest to them. When kids are surrounded by their peers all the time, they tend to be persuaded to follow their ways, even if some of them aren't making the best choices. Parents tend to be seen as "out of touch". If their moms and dads are the ones guiding and training them through these tumultuous years, children are less likely to turn outwardly for value and acceptance. Parents retain their credibility by being their children's primary teachers, as well, because there are much fewer conflicting worldviews vying for their children's hearts and minds. Your child isn't wondering why his or her teacher and friends at school all seem to say one thing, and you say the exact opposite.

Distance in a relationship with a child can be overcome through taking a genuine interest in their interests, working to figure out problems together. It much easier to connect with your kids when you already spend a great deal of time with them. Teenagers don't rebel against authority, they rebel against a lack of relationship. Voddie Baucham, Jr. states in his 2007 book *Family Driven Faith*, "The retention rate [of kids who stay in the church] is not highest among those in youth groups; it is highest among those whose parents (particularly fathers) actually disciple them." Siblings aren't separated from each other into different classrooms during the day, either, so they grow close and learn to cooperate. They learn to work out their conflicts with one another, because they have no other choice. My children don't always get along perfectly, but they prefer to spend time with each other than with anybody else.

There is also an enormous academic benefit to children who are educated at home, contrary to what education administrators and the liberal media tell you. As the previous chapters in this book have outlined, the substandard learning methods and curricula of government run schools continue to fail millions of children in America. A nationwide study by Dr. Brian Ray, an internationally recognized scholar and president of the non-profit National Home Education Research Institute (NHERI), provides a definitive answer to the question of whether homeschooled kids do better than those in public school. Drawing from 15 independent testing services, his *Progress Report 2009:*

Homeschool Academic Achievement and Demographics included 11,739 homeschooled students from all 50 states who took three well-known tests- California Achievement Test, Iowa Tests of Basic Skills, and Stanford Achievement Test- for the 2007-2008 academic year.

The overall results of the study showed significant advances in homeschool academic achievement, and revealed that issues such as student gender, parents' education level, and family income had little bearing on the results. Whether either parent was a certified teacher did not matter, either. Children scored in the 87th percentile having a parent who was certified, and in the 88th percentile with neither parent ever having been certified. Parental spending on home education made little difference also. When parents spent $600 or more on the student, the child scored in the 89th percentile, compared to the 86th when parental spending was under $600. The national average percentile scores for public schooled students, by comparison, was just 50 in all subtests.

Because of the time, money, and energy you invest in your children's lives, you will also be providing the public with one healthy family, comprised of well-adjusted, productive individuals. Economists tell us

135

that the difficult work of childrearing provides a benefit to society, called "positive fiscal externality", since those children will not grow up to become dependent upon the state. From my years of working with different populations depending on social welfare, I can say with confidence that the system is hopelessly, irreversibly broken. Welfare, another massive government run program like education, will not fix the magnitude of problems this country is facing.

  Ultimately, homeschooling mothers and fathers save the state money by taking care of their own dependent young, rather than foisting that responsibility onto the taxpayers. These teachers build human capital, without making demands on budget-conscious appropriators already besieged with requests from competing interests. Before the mid-19th century in America, the family and the church assumed the responsibility of caring for the people. It's high time to get back to those days. A large, centralized government with all of its spending and programs has proved that it fails to adequately address the nation's myriad of troubling issues. In fact, it creates these very problems of fragmented families, immorality, and poverty through illiteracy at the front end through public education, and then presumes to offer the solutions at the back end with social "welfare". It perpetuates a hopeless cycle of dependency on government.

You may be thinking at this point: this all sounds great, but how do I begin? Around two million families homeschool in America, so you are in great company. Data from the National Center for Education Statistics measured a 74% increase in homeschooling from 2001 to 2009- twelve times the increase of public school students over the same period.[55] There are countless curricula available these days from a wide variety of Christian publishers. There are resources such as learning co-ops that could help you succeed in teaching subject areas where you feel weak, support groups, websites, and legal support (should you ever need it) through HSLDA (Home School Legal Defense Association). Pinterest has no shortage of unit studies, along with crafts, games, and activities to enhance your child's education. Homeschooling is legal in all 50 states, but the procedure for getting started varies from state to state. To find out the exact procedure for getting started in your home state, as well as tips on every aspect of

---

[55] Robert Kunzman, "Write These Laws On Your Children: Inside the World of Conservative Christian Homeschooling" (Boston, MA: Beacon Press), 2009.

homeschooling, visit HSLDA's website: www.hslda.org.

There are so many curriculum choices available these days that it can be a bit overwhelming selecting the right one for your child(ren). I personally recommend Sonlight, My Father's World, or A Beka. These are all excellent because of their biblical and academic lessons and materials. The most important thing to keep in mind when trying to decide which curriculum to use is, will this fit the needs of my child and our family? Maybe your child would benefit more from a hands-on approach, or maybe he or she prefers workbooks. You can buy pre-packaged curriculum that comes with ready-made lesson plans, so you don't have to do all the planning yourself. With those lesson plans comes the flexibility of customizing it for your individual child, too. You could also combine materials from two or more curricula; language arts and science from one, math from another.

Once you have chosen your curriculum, you should establish a daily schedule. Think through what order you would like to teach each subject, and what time of day is best for both you and your children. You do not have to organize your day to fit with the regular 8am to 2:30pm school schedule. The average length of "seat time" instruction for homeschoolers is about 3 hours per day. You have the freedom to take large breaks in between each subject, or do them all in the morning right after breakfast! Most times, you will find you can probably combine subjects like Geography and Science, or Language Arts and History. Of course, a set time for Bible reading and Scripture memorization is important, but remember that the goal of a biblical education is to have each subject underscored by a biblical worldview. That means we teach History, Science, etc. through the lens of our "biblical glasses", as the founder of apologetics ministry Answers in Genesis, Ken Ham, would say.

Decide also whether you want to accomplish school five days a week, or four with a day set aside for field trips or a co-op. A schedule is important because it provides a guide for each day, but it shouldn't be a task master either. Sometimes, due to the circumstances, it will be necessary to change things around, or scrap everything entirely. It is just as important to be realistic when putting together a schedule. Plan, but also be flexible!

Most important of all is letting go of expectations and giving yourself grace. It is no small task to educate, train, and disciple your children. It can be even more difficult if they have been in the public school system for some time, making the adjustment to a home education. When we began homeschooling, I had the support of our family and many friends, along with a great homeschool group at our church, but to be honest my heart just wasn't in it. I felt as if this was a door slamming shut on a future I had all planned out. I was nervous that I was going to mess up my kid, and scared that I wouldn't be able to give my daughter the attention that she needed at the same time. I worried how I would possibly educate a six-year-old, entertain a three-year-old, *and* do the laundry, prepare meals, and keep the house clean. In short, I didn't believe that I was the right person for the job.

There were moments of sheer frustration when my son struggled to blend sounds together to form words, and I believed he would never learn to read. There were times I thought I would lose my mind when he couldn't figure out how to count sequentially past twenty. However, the rewards were great when he finally had those breakthroughs! The best part was simply being there every step of the way to encourage him and see him succeed. Before I knew it, he was flying through his phonics readers and wanting to try

Dr. Seuss books. I blinked, and he counted to 200 all by himself. Those are things I will treasure forever.

It turns out that I had underestimated myself, and my kid. Instead of having to keep pace with the rest of his class, my son was able to concentrate on the areas where he needed a little more help. He also had the freedom to delve more into a subject he excelled at, or that he was just really interested in. He could also learn using the style that suited him best. Being very hands-on, he naturally absorbed material at home through acting out something we read, manipulating objects, and plain old exploring.

There are definitely still some days that we struggle through, because of frustration over certain assignments, or because my children are tired and irritable. Sometimes it is difficult to manage teaching along with all the laundry, dishes, and house cleaning. I have learned, however, to rely on God for the strength and patience I do not naturally have, and direct my kids to do the same. I have also learned to start enlisting my children's help with chores, though they don't always do them the "correct" way. They learn responsibility and teamwork, and more gets accomplished when everyone pitches in. It helps to take play breaks, or head outside with all the books and materials to the backyard or park, if they are becoming frustrated and having trouble focusing.

I know that the decision to provide a biblical education at home for your children can be intimidating. You might have to sacrifice considerable money, time, and energy. You might not think that you are up for the task, but God will provide exactly what you need to fulfill the Great Commission in your own home! Through His church, He will equip you for this ministry (Ephesians 4:11-13). By His Spirit He will empower you (Acts 1:8), and He Himself will be with you to fulfill this calling (Matthew 28:20). In addition, He has given you His Word to sanctify you (John 17:17) and to fully equip you for every good work (2 Timothy 3:16-17).

I should point out here that homeschooling in and of itself is not a formula for producing godly children. It is a biblical mandate, but as with any other ministry, the results are not guaranteed. Our responsibility is to be obedient and plant those seeds of faith, while God waters the seeds. We must be careful that our lives and our doctrine also match each other. Homeschooling is really 99% parenting, and 1% teaching! If we concentrate all of our efforts on curriculum, we will be missing the mark. Modeling a life of service and obedience to the Lord before our children shows them that they can believe in the power of the Gospel. Otherwise, they may have an appearance of godliness, but deny its power (2 Timothy 3:5). Home education is not their salvation; they have only one Savior, and that is Jesus Christ.

Certainly we can do better than a government controlled education that undermines the family and the church at every turn with humanistic teachings, and which deliberately dumbs down students. The alternative of homeschooling is an extremely effective way to influence your children for Christ, away from harmful attitudes and instruction. It ensures the passing down of the tradition of faith from generation to generation, keeping the individualistic spirit alive. The current approach of sending Christian kids to public schools isn't working. Our children are being sacrificed on the altar of relationship evangelism, with absolutely catastrophic results. In our current condition, the overwhelming majority of youth are leaving the church visible by the end of their freshman year in college.

We must make the necessary sacrifices and adjustments if we want to change the course of events. God has given us as parents the awesome responsibility of preparing our children to be launched from our homes as arrows aimed at the kingdom of darkness. It requires a complete lifestyle and worldview overhaul, but it will pay out incredible dividends for this world, and for eternity.

> *Let it be remembered, that I do not speak to the wild, giddy, thoughtless world, but to those that fear God. I ask, then, for what end do you send your children to school? Why? That they may be fit to live in the world? In which world do you mean, — this or the next? Perhaps you thought of this world only; and had forgot that there is a world to come; yea, and one that will last forever! Pray take this into your account, and send them to such masters as will keep it always before their eyes. Otherwise, to send them to school (permit me to speak plainly) is little better than sending them to the devil. At all events, then, send your boys [and girls], if you have any concern for their souls, not to any of the large public schools, (for they are nurseries of all manner of wickedness,) but private school, kept by some pious man, who endeavors to instruct a small number of children in religion and learning together. - John Wesley*

For Further Reading

Homeschooling 101: A Guide To Getting Started by Erica Arndt
Family Driven Faith by Voddie Baucham, Jr.
Crimes of the Educators by Samuel Blumenfeld & Alex Newman
Dumbing Us Down: The Hidden Curriculum of Compulsory Schooling by John Taylor Gatto
Already Gone by Ken Ham
The Deliberate Dumbing Down Of America by Charlotte Iserbyt
Culture Shift: Engaging Current Issues With Timeless Truth by Albert Mohler
The Harsh Truth About Public Schools by Bruce Shortt
Full-Time Parenting: A Guide To Family-Based Discipleship by Israel Wayne

About The Author

Marisa Boonstra received her Masters degree in Social Work from Rutgers University. She is a wife and homeschooling mother of two, who is passionate about encouraging women to find purpose and joy in their God-given calling as mothers, and helping them raise children with a biblical worldview. Her website is calledtomothering.com

To Contact Marisa

email: marisa.boonstra@calledtomothering.com

Mailing Address:
Marisa Boonstra
12101 North MacArthur Boulevard
Suite 256
Oklahoma City, Oklahoma 73162

Made in the USA
Coppell, TX
11 May 2022